ENGLISH
ELEGANCE

ENGLISH ELEGANCE

JUDY BRITTAIN / PATRICK KINMONTH

HOLT, RINEHART AND WINSTON

NEW YORK

This book is dedicated to the houses, their owners and to these photographers
who took the pictures

Timothy Beddow · Eric Boman · Christopher Drake · Kenneth
Griffiths · Lucinda Lambton · David Montgomery · Derry Moore ·
James Mortimer · Snowdon · Christopher Simon Sykes · Tessa Traeger

*Frontispiece: The sixteenth-century stencil and fresco
trompe-l'oeil staircase at the Villa Cicogna, Varese.*

Copyright © 1984 by The Conde Nast Publications Ltd

First published in the United States in 1985 by
Holt, Rinehart and Winston, 383 Madison Avenue,
New York, New York 10017.

Originally published in Great Britain under the title *Living in Vogue*.

Library of Congress Cataloging in Publication Data

Brittain, Judy.
English elegance.

1. Interior decoration – Great Britain – History –
20th century. I. Kinmonth, Patrick. II. Title.
NK2403.B75   1984   728'.092'2   85-8448

ISBN: 0-03-005854-6

First American Edition

Designed by Barney Wan and Elizabeth Wickham

Colour Reproduction by Adroit Photo-Litho Ltd., Birmingham
Printed in Spain by
Printer industria grafica s.a. Barcelona
D.L.B. 22336 - 1984
1   3   5   7   9   10   8   6   4   2

CONTENTS

INTRODUCTION

'There is a Lordship of the Eye which being a raunging, and imperious Sence, can indure no narrow circumspection; but must be fed both with extent and varietie, that agreeable harmony between the length, breadth and height of all the rooms, which suddenly, where it is, taketh every beholder by the secret power of proportion . . .'

H. Wotton, *Elements of Architecture* 1624

This book is about houses. From outside in and inside out, it is about the spirit of some marvellous places and how to come to some agreement with your surroundings by looking into the houses and ideas of people who definitely have done so. Over ten years there have been many. Big, small, historic, mythical, mellowed with age, as bright as new paint; cottages, flats; some highly and artfully decorated, some just lived in and become beautiful with the living. They all share one thing in common, that they breathe with the people who live there or have lived there in the past. Mere taste and design are meaningless without this contribution which makes the places hum, sing and buzz.

Each has its own particular character, either felt through its architecture, as in Palladian villas in the Veneto, or through the odd conglomeration of paraphernalia collected through a life or lives, or equally because people who speak the language of the eye – artists and designers – have brought to them their own sense of colour, line and harmony. There are also the houses owned by people who are in their particular way eccentric. As Henry Moore once remarked, 'If I am abnormal that may be my contribution to society'; and the eccentricity in surroundings is one of this book's chief delights. Other owners have passions for a particular thing and their collections give their houses a rich and contagious enthusiasm.

To be beautiful, form must follow function. This tenet of the modern movement is acceptable as far as it goes but form need not stop there. Decoration is the continuation of a process of architecture. When function and form have both been satisfied the fun can start, the game of finding which colour, which objects, which arrangements will suit the place as well as the people living there. The houses in this book are a study in temperament. There are romantic rooms; architectural rooms; cool sophisticates, all silver, olive, green and beige; jazzy wits, all pattern and colour; untidy rooms, with peeling walls; the deceptively simple and the frankly mad – a catalogue of variety. The rooms of show-offs, dreamers, hermits, gossips, cooks, writers, artists, the famous and the unknown. Such variations can satisfy two instincts: curiosity, since you can snoop with a clear conscience, and the need for change. Most important, the individuality of these houses should urge us to think for ourselves rather than blindly follow the latest fashion in interior design, which may be quite misplaced in our own lives.

The Villa Poiana by Andrea Palladio.

In the sixteenth century Palladio produced some of the happiest and most serene of houses in Italy. They combine the fruits of his labours, painstaking days spent measuring the remaining classical buildings of ancient Rome, with an extraordinary understanding of human scale. They are stately without being pompous but, as Nikolaus Pevsner points out, their significance lies in their relationship to their surroundings. The low outbuildings take in the land around and 'This embracing attitude proved of the greatest historical consequence. Here for the first time in Western architecture landscape and building were conceived of as belonging to each other, as dependent on each other.' The houses Palladio built, even in dereliction, have an unsurpassed beauty of form and a marvellous play of shape and light. Sir Christopher Wren's description of Salisbury cathedral, written in about 1669, could equally well be applied to Palladio's villas: 'The windows are not made too great, nor yet the Light obstructed with many mullions; our artist knew better that nothing could add Beauty to Light, he trusted to a stately and rich Plainness.' The principles of Palladio, however loftily conceived, have their application in all houses. By looking at the perfection of his symmetry we can see that proportion exists as a priority even when it is absent. We may have only a few small, mean rooms, but there is no reason why we should not all be Palladian in our manipulation of space and light.

Style and taste are like perfect manners; they cannot be taught but they can be copied, dealing as they do with insight and the intuition that transforms the good into the rare. But we should not be too holy in our masters. The English have erred too often into the safe waters of good taste rather than playing more exciting games with the pirate ship of bad, sometimes because we have not managed to meet the wrong people. A number of the people in this book have abandoned convention in favour of their own instincts. Their houses are as revealing as any painting but they need to be looked at carefully before their secrets reveal themselves to innocent eyes. It may be the intuition of Craigie Aitchison, the painter, that discovers a value and quality in cheap bits and pieces, rich in sentiment, or which keeps a cake on the kitchen table to look at rather than to eat, or the house of Michael Cardew, the potter, who has let the walls darken to a rich brown with smoke from the fire and the work of twenty years' weathering. More obvious lessons are to be drawn from professionals who have made it their life's work to make the places in which people live, work. The book teaches through photography: the treatment of fabric, from elaborate tasselled draperies to a single stretch of muslin tacked over a window to filter the light; the use of colour, showing the combinations that a life spent working on room design has finally produced – the wonderful clashing reds of David Hicks' rooms in Piccadilly, the sixteen tones of white that David Mlinaric used at Beningbrough in Yorkshire, or the classic yellows, greys and sands of the decorators' vocabulary; solutions to floors – painted, often with daring patterns, broken up with rugs or simple raffia mats, hardly ever with fitted carpets; ideas for walls, ceilings, doors, halls, bedrooms, back-rooms, pantries and porches . . .

If Palladio's houses have a dreamlike quality it is partly because they seem to belong to some endless summer. There is good reason for this. They were built as an escape in hot months from the stifling canals of Venice and were designed for golden afternoons. In his enthusiasm, Lord Burlington overlooked this when he built a copy of Palladio's Villa Rotunda in Chiswick in the eighteenth century and froze there in splendour. We must not be slavish in our imitations, nor mind a few loose ends; so much of the art of decoration lies in supplying just enough to get the imagination working without caring too much about what happens behind the scenes. In an ideal world all wiring would be hidden, all switches perfectly placed, all lighting designed for one person's needs. But that applies only to one kind of house.

Perhaps the final function of the book is as a catalyst to dreams. Cyril Connolly had a marvellous one in his book *The Unquiet Grave*. 'Daydream: a golden classical house, three stories high, with attic windows and a view over water. Outside a magnolia growing up the wall, a terrace for winter, a great tree for summer and a lawn for games; behind it a wooded hill and in front a river, then a sheltered garden, indulgent to fig and nectarine.' No mention of paint, carpets, light fittings, yet a whole house stands before us. How easily we could walk across that lawn, and the other lawns in this book, in the late evening light, with the sound of a mower somewhere and voices. Inside are vases of flowers, great sprays, peonies, colours you can smell on sight, a pile of books, a tea-tray, a chaotically ordered desk. Postcards stick out from behind the clock on the mantelpiece – one of those amazing affairs with golden figures holding bows and arrows, chins propped on wrists, dwelling on time as it passes. We might go further. Into a dark and shiny passage to a kitchen all simmering pans and lemonade in white jugs, or across a hard, echoing hall with its lantern and its grandfather clock where, as the hour strikes, a ship rocks on a painted sea . . .

Façade of the Villa Poiana, abandoned to wind, weeds and chickens.

A still life of Chinese pots with Michael Szell's peony silk and real peonies.

THE PROFESSIONAL EYE

'Taste is at present the darling idol of the polite world, and indeed, seems to be considered as the quintessence of almost all the arts and sciences.'

The Connoisseur, 13 May 1756

Much of the work of an interior designer is invisible. It goes on behind walls, below floors and above ceilings. The evident things, finish, colour, choice of objects and pattern are only part of the skills of the best, who are often closer to architects than they are to decorators. Whereas in the past architecture has shown itself to be deeply concerned with decoration, in recent decades it has been more involved with the possibilities of construction in new materials. In the hands of its masters this produced some of the most radical design of the century but it encouraged the unfortunate notion that decoration on buildings lacked integrity because impact should rely on dynamic structure alone. This false notion of purity is being dispelled and a more fruitful bond between architecture and decoration seems possible. After all, a look at Ancient Egypt's painted temples, the Parthenon marbles, the frescos at Pompeii and the many flowerings of the centuries between shows the idea to be neither new nor bad.

Some of the most beautiful statements of design in this book are to do with building. Roderick Cameron's marvel of a staircase, twisting up like a nautilus shell at the end of a light-washed corridor in Provence, and most marked of all, John Stefanidis' conversion of farm buildings from nineteenth-century sheds into an informal version of the classic house in a landscape around the geometry of a courtyard. Rarely will a designer of this calibre be engaged only to advise on paint and paper. Their principal work lies in the re-arrangement of a given space so that it will fit as exactly as possible the needs of the person who is to live there. For this reason it is in the houses that these designers have made for themselves that the clearest idea of their tastes can be seen. Certain similarities emerge. Where the architecture is good to begin with, there is a shared concern to respect and restore it. There is a preference in most cases for local materials, as well as for furniture and things that bear a direct relation to the house, where it is and anything that makes it very much itself. In David Mlinaric's house in East Anglia all the basic fittings were brought from local builders, whilst the colours chosen, soft grey and bleak blue, the light of huge skies, let the original mood of the place speak. Christopher Gibbs strips his house to the bone, then fills it with a cast of characters, furniture and objects that suit his antiquarian and romantic sense of the past. When working for other people the skill of the best interior designers should be noticeable only as an atmosphere. The rooms should speak about their owners, not about their designers. In some of their own houses, the designers play games with their own skills and the arrangement of objects becomes formalised to the point where it is a professional flourish. Sometimes their work will border on the theatrical, with references to many other places, until the house is almost disguised, like John Fowler's later Nicholas Haslam's, mock-Jacobean folly in Hampshire.

Another rather surprising fact is that most of these designers have not changed the houses that they live in very much over the years. Not for them the tearing down of pelmets and the hammering up of swagged blinds in a fever of fashion; they tend to know what they want and settle for it. This constancy is part of their conviction. They are sure where you are uncertain, they can foresee what you have not imagined.

JOHN STEFANIDIS

A Suite of Rooms in Chelsea
Converted Farm Buildings in Dorset

'I own I like definite form in what my eyes are to rest upon; and if landscapes were sold, like the sheets of characters of my boyhood, one penny plain and twopence coloured, I should go to the length of twopence every day of my life . . .'

Robert Louis Stevenson

Like Stevenson in his *Travels with a Donkey in the Cevennes*, John Stefanidis sees with a clearer eye, freed from the constraints of living in the country in which he was born and the landscapes that he inhabited as a child in Egypt and Greece. He has chosen for himself a series of pale and perfectly proportioned rooms in London, and in Dorset a perfectly proportioned landscape of hedge, wood and smooth hills in which he made a house from old cowsheds. More than an interior designer is allowed to be by popular consent, and what an architect should be (but seldom is) by popular demand, Stefanidis is something of a misfit. His sense of form and texture is that of the painter. His work, when

Left: The stencilled sitting-room: designed for eyes to travel over the different strengths of colour on the walls painted by Harry Gremillion to imitate the quality of an oriental textile on which the pictures, engravings, have been hung for their colours, cool grey and sepia, no more important than the walls behind them. A row of silver pots are a formal study in repetition, in contrast to the exuberant cymbidian orchids. The leather-edged shelves continue the perfect finish on all surfaces. The sofa is covered with a rice-patterned Stefanidis cotton, with cushions of wild carnation silk, also a Stefanidis design.

Overleaf: The big room, used as a dining-room facing the river and full of reflected light. The roman blinds of white stuff are draped in appropriate proportion to the bay window, neither full nor mean, and soften the light around the dining-table with its deeply cushioned window seat. In the foreground a giant stool by Stefanidis suggested by an Indian design. Above the fireplace carvings reminiscent of Grinling Gibbons are boldly painted white. On the far wall hangs an outsized painting by Cy Twombly, at home with things from the past, whilst the parquet floor is spaced with rugs, their colours muted and eloquent with age.

Top left: The house seen from the lawn.

Middle: The back hall with Dorset tile floor. Painted chest by Rose Yorke. Here, as in the rest of the house, the heating system is cased inside slatted wooden frames, sometimes cushioned as window seats.

Left: Main guest bedroom with a brick floor in basket pattern partly covered with a bright rug. The bed is hung with white cotton pique and lined with Farfall fabric designed by John Stefanidis.

Above: In the kitchen, at the opposite end from the small sitting-room, the lowered ceiling makes a distinction with the rest of the space. A table by John Makepeace seats sixteen, the plates are by Millington-Drake. Kitchen equipment is cloistered inside tiled surrounds.

you sit inside it or walk from room to room, has the effect of art first, craft second. This can only be achieved from a working method that has a clear sense of purpose.

To be in a Stefanidis house is to be extremely comfortable. It gives the lie to the belief that comfort means comfortable sofas, although he designs those too; large areas are left empty and their proportions are as relaxing to look at as his furniture is to sit on. 'If we lived in another country we would be building all the time, whole complexes of buildings like our work for Patmos and Mustique. This does of course involve a lot of building itself, but since it looks completely natural when we have finished, the extent of work is not realised. What we care about is the logic of a space and the practicality of a design as much as appearance, texture and finish.' A group of dilapidated Victorian cowsheds may not at first seem the best material for making into a home, but John Stefanidis would rather work on that 'than a third-rate Georgian house', which is the Londoner's usual country retreat. The key to the success of the conversion is that, from the beginning, Stefanidis was determined not to make the house pretty and self-conscious; in the best traditions of treating old buildings,

the existing character was enhanced and the result is far from contrived, uncomfortable or primitive. The buildings are examples of straightforward late-Victorian farm architecture: brick, with occasional touches of decorative woodwork; the most elaborate part is the detached (and unconverted) structure, which was possibly used for lambing, and which has elegant arched brick walls and half-timbered gables. There never was a farmhouse here: only the small building near the entrance was remotely habitable, for it had a fireplace and was probably used as a shelter for the cow-hands.

When John Stefanidis arrived the cows had long gone; the buildings were derelict and being used for storage. All the work has been carried out very conservatively. The roof keeps its horizontal 'polychromy' – the Victorian word for striping in different materials – and the other slate roofs are retained. All the woodwork has been carefully repaired or replaced and – most happily – creosoted black, so that the no-nonsense and genuinely rural character of the buildings is still paramount. The house looks inward to the courtyard; by the road the rugged blank façade has been preserved largely unaltered to secure protection from agricultural noise and passers-by. A structure designed for the comfort of cows is not, however, necessarily ideal for the needs of human beings. A new building had to be placed at the far end of the yard connecting the two principal parallel wings. Here, Stefanidis' sensitivity is very evident, for the infill is low, of wood, with its windows and eaves continuing the levels set by the long tiled wing on the right, while the new roof is of slate, like those on the opposite side. The wood is painted black with the window and door frames white, or blue on the side of the field. The windows were a problem. The cowsheds originally had openings filled with two sections of vertical slats – one sliding, one fixed. By replacing the inner panel with glass and keeping the outer fixed slats, a most effective and practical treatment has been achieved, which lets in plenty of light and creates a necessary and attractive screen. On the garden front – overlooking the fields – new windows

had to be invented. 'It was tricky not to make them pretentious,' says Stefanidis, that is, with too many Georgian glazing-bars; instead, square windows divided into four strike just the right note of rustic simplicity. The entrance to the house is at the opposite end of the long yard, which has been most carefully arranged and planted. The first part is an orchard; beyond is a pattern of paths and box and lavender hedges. The spaces are generous and – by being all on one level – seem so much grander and more luxurious than if on two floors. There are vistas, as the spaces interconnect, but they are broken up by changes in direction and by the new double-sided chimney piece, which, being centrally placed between the small sitting-room and the drawing-room, allows openings either side which relate, *en enfilade*, with other doors. These spaces are articulated and given appropriate character by differing ceiling heights – low and more intimate in the bedrooms, higher for the communal rooms, where the roof structure of beams and tie-rods is exposed – but not too many beams, as Stefanidis happily notes. Slightly rough plaster in the bedrooms, white-painted brickwork elsewhere but not dead white; tinted with pink or yellow. This subtlety is evident in the themes which run through the house, such as the window details, the brick floors (laid in different patterns), and radiator covers of painted wooden slats. In the furnishing there is a prevalence of light muted colours; comfortable, rather geometrical furniture; rugs and matting on the brick floors; carefully disposed pieces of antique furniture and Oriental art. It is all very convenient.

The house in London is a variation upon themes. A suite of high, pale rooms on the first floor, overlooking the river, their palette borrows from different sources. The walls of the small sitting-room are stencilled with the most sophisticated patterns to imitate a faded textile, the main room is flooded with light bounced off the Thames, which makes its own pattern on the walls. His style is addictive, its creaminess, the balancing act of faded colour and clean line, a spartan inflection and a pleasing opulence of atmosphere which sets his work apart.

Left: The 'long gallery', built to connect the two original buildings, has carpets designed by Teddy Millington-Drake. The library bookcases are built from floor to ceiling, their vertical lines emphasising the room's height in the classical manner and framing the view to the small sitting-room which leads into the large one pictured overleaf. Brick walls are washed white with a hint of pink, windows are plainly shuttered, not curtained.

Overleaf: In the large sitting-room, once a cowshed, the original architecture is enhanced, beams laid bare, simple windows added to face those onto the courtyard, a brick floor laid, part-covered with rush matting. At the far end double-doors lead to the main bedroom and bathroom. The whole an essay in simplicity on the grand scale.

CHRISTOPHER GIBBS
The Story of Davington Priory in Kent

Christopher Gibbs has an eye that sees more than most people. He sees the poignant threads of history in a faded damask or a curious shoe, last vestige of some famous foot, the chair that bore the weight of a poet, the tapestry that was privy to whispered secrets. His romantic vision of objects is his great strength, nowhere more evident than in his search for and ten-year romance with an ancient and secret place – Davington Priory.

'The first time I saw Davington it was a raw April morning. Above the stonework rose the gabled front painted pink, with the woodwork and the untidy mess of drainpipes battleship grey. An apron of gravel stretched before it to trim lawn, marred by diamond-shaped beds, neatly planted. Beyond this, iron railings enclosed a paddock centred by a proud walnut tree and fringed by a narrow belt of shabby woodland just now sprouting fresh and green. I stepped into the tiled hall, lit by its double lancet of stained glass, and walked slowly round the house. The decorations were tawdry – Indian restaurant flock in the drawing-room, whose tall windows looked down to the pond and the new housing estate. The cloister, shining pink, ended in a blank and newly plastered wall, where the Norman archway led into the church but looked out through windows with pretty shields of painted glass echoing the wallflowers dabbed with flecks of brilliant tulips in their patterned box hedges outside. The dining-room, thickly painted shiny blue and black, did its best to disguise the beauty and strangeness of its Jacobean stone mantel, and the Gothic text "May Health, Peace and Grace abyde in this place" could still be seen over the door. Up the carved oak staircase, with its grimacing lion finials, was a warren of little rooms, but I could see the stone chimney pieces and the seventeenth-century panelling through their thickly choking mask of dirty paint, and everywhere light fell through painted shields and saints. I think I was there for twenty minutes, and two days later I bought the priory at a crowded auction in a Maidstone hotel.

'For a year I lived there, familiarising myself with the house's history, scratching paint, moving my base from room to room as the tale unravelled; making friends with Ken Judges, gardener there for twenty-five years, the priory's constant cherisher and guardian; with the Bunting brothers, who ruled the allotments, ponds and weirs that made my view across the road, beneath the spine of the old town and the wooded hills of the Blean, where, on the wet stones of the nuns' fishponds, gunpowder had been

Above: Davington Priory with the Norman tower rising above the painted clapboard façade of the inner courtyard.

Right: Christopher Gibbs, the antique dealer and writer, seated in a grotto chair in the ante-room to the library. Outsize books flank a full-length portrait but are overshadowed by lilies in an appropriately tall lily vase.

milled since the sixteenth century. I made friends at church and opened, with my own hands, the door that joined God's house with my own.

'I learned that the Priory of St Mary Magdalene at Davington was founded on a site already occupied for a thousand years by Benedictine nuns from Cluny in 1153. During the tenure of the Cheynes in the reign of Henry VIII the house began to take the form it has now. The cloister with its splendid moulded chestnut beams was enclosed. The row of gables was raised and garnished with grinning masks, the church sheered in half, the northernmost of the twin towers toppled. Despite being used to shelter the ewes at lambing time and to store poles from the priory hop garden, the church was always swept and clean for the feasts, going ever so gently downhill until it was rescued by Thomas Willement, stained glass maker, herald and antiquary, who in the 1840s restored with care and enlarged with thoughtfulness both church and house. He made the garden, glazed the windows with old painted roundels and shields and patterns of his own devising, kept up the manorial courts and appointed his priests. When his daughter died, it was sold and ten years later bought, together with its ancient rights and privileges, by the Church of England, who re-dedicated the church and sold me the house.

'Then came the year of the wand. My friend Nicky Johnston, architect, and the able workmen of Wiltshires, the old Canterbury firm of builders, bore the brunt of the work. The stained glass that had been removed by the diocese was returned and shone with new brilliance. The lordship of the manor with its vellum rolls and the beautiful books of the priory's history that Willement made, with their before and after water-colours and their faded callotypes, came home in the bishop's boot. Reg Saxby and his son Paul gilded the cross and weather-vane. Ken handed me the keys of the priory clocks wrought as a prior's staff with a big D, and the house was flayed, scraped, banged and

In Davington Priory it is the furniture, paintings, objects and textiles which provide the decoration rather than the wall and window treatment or the upholstery. (The leaded windows, inset with stained glass, throw dapples of colour on the rug-covered floor.) Here in the library, Oriental textiles and Moroccan cushions pile up on the chair and on the daybed which once belonged to Lord Tennyson. In the distance an English nineteenth-century dummy-board dog, a medieval lance against the wall, African stools, piles of books, large pots and many postcards, flowers and water-lilies in a horn cup.

plumbed, sparked, plastered and painted – and rose refreshed while Ken turfed over beds and gravel and painted the grass with drifts of purple hyacinths and pheasant's-eye narcissi, and made ramparts of old roses and a green room with a wall of winter-flowering viburnum. Foresters cleared fallen trees and hacked out suckering saplings and John East picked out hundreds of tree stumps. Groves and hedges were planted and peopled with antique marbles and blossom and flourish. Within, Oriental carpets, worn pools of colour, warmed bleached and waxed boards. Moorish silks were hung at the windows and simple and extraordinary furniture furnished the empty rooms. A little later Joan and Doreen came up to polish and shine and clean the house. Mrs Wagland came up to cook delicious food and look after me. Family and friends came to stay, encouraging and delighting. A reign of harmony seemed to stretch before me.

'Painted in faded black letters on the weatherboarding inside the carved cloister porch is the legend:

> Nec Mihi
> Mox Huius
> Sed Postea Nescio Cuius

which I take to mean loosely: "Now mine, then theirs, but forever after I know not whose."'

Above: The dining-room where the Victorian Gothic windows are left uncurtained and the floors bare. The plain painted eighteenth-century English table is offset with unusual loop-backed chairs of the same period by Robert Mainwaring.

Right: The upstairs sitting-room. Japanese clothes rack hung with antique clothes, silk curtains from Morocco, a Ming jar on John Evelyn's giant slice of oak table, Moroccan rug, elk antlers, red chair circa 1700.

Top: In the bathroom painted wooden casings for bath and basin are the same as the little cupboard by the window with stained glass insets. A comfortable horsehair chair and the cushioned window-seat make this a sociable sitting-room/bathroom.

Above: An oak-panelled bedroom at the end of a long corridor with embroidered hanging and an oak bed.

Right: The main bedroom where everything is as plain as possible except for the window which is mostly Flemish seventeenth-century stained glass.

DAVID HICKS
Red Rooms in Piccadilly

David Hicks' chambers in Albany, London's first gentleman's lodgings in Piccadilly, represent his work in miniature, his ideas of colour and notions of scale. He is ruled by a sense of geometry, whilst his colour sense, which has often seemed to rely for its effects on sophisticated unnaturalness, is in fact drawn from the range of tones that exists in the natural world. The shades of red upon red upon red that form a complex relationship in his London rooms find their counterpart in the outside world, like a green garden whose colours, upon close inspection, veer from acid yellow-greens to sumptuous mints and olives. For Hicks (and perhaps for all designers) what seems artificial is only a transformation of what occurs naturally elsewhere in another form. The smallness of the rooms in Albany is disguised by using a mirror from ceiling to floor, breaking down the limited space. Instead of relying on the walls to dictate, certain major pieces of furniture and rare objects are daringly placed, like the great draped bed which takes centre stage in the bedroom.

Left: The drawing-room, filled with gilded furniture and beautiful objects, is in itself a master class on colour, where a fuschia chair, edged with gold, sits in harmony against flame walls. To enlarge the room a ceiling-high mirror reflects to eternity a Reynolds portrait hung from a scarlet sash.

Above: David Hicks at breakfast in his Albany chambers, a complex of rooms unified with many shades of red.

Sometimes the two concerns – rare objects, elusive space – combine, as in the hanging of a Reynolds portrait on top of a mirror wall, where it sits as if in mid-air. A pleasant growth of books and cuttings, postcards and letters softens the lines. 'One only really sees a room the first time one enters it. Like any room that works well, it disappears after you know it properly.' What never disappears is something that is wrong. The test of good English design is linked with the ethic (of which David Hicks is a good example) of the best-dressed Englishman: their tailoring is so appropriate that it disappears, not because it is drab but because it is exactly in the image of its wearer.

Left: The bedroom seen from the drawing-room. The great, canopied bed holds centre stage and beyond it the mirrored chimney-breast reflects and doubles the space. The walls are precisely punctuated with pictures.

Above: The clerk's desk, which faces the bed, is a small autobiography in its choice of books, from 'Mountbatten' (a biography of his father-in-law) to titles on Egypt and the eighteenth century. Somehow they manage to be the books he needs and still have predominantly red covers. A photograph of Noël Coward (a family friend) looks on. Near the desk a glimpse of violet chair. Behind the desk decoratively bunched curtains let in the light.

BENINGBROUGH

Restoration of a Great House in Yorkshire

A clear shape of soft red brick, Beningbrough Hall stands out like an impeccable water-colour drawing from a stretch of flat Yorkshire countryside. The bricks are local, made from the alluvial clay of the River Ouse, but the inspired and eclectic decoration of the house, the work of William Thornton, a Yorkshire carpenter–cum–master builder, looks to Baroque Italy in the young eighteenth century for its eccentric solutions.

Completed in 1716, its beauty lies in Thornton's curious details of carving that are everywhere, set upon the face of a severely lineal and restrained architecture, like the surprising window frame with 'ears' that surmounts the front door, a borrowing from Bernini's Palazzo Chigi in Rome. Within, the house's greatest distinction is its hall and the marvellously generous stone-flagged corridors, which cut across its centre. It was in the hall that David Mlinaric began the immense task of restoration at Beningbrough for the National Trust, to consolidate its standing as one of the greatest Baroque houses in England.

'We thought we would start here because it was the most difficult, and because it was the most interesting room architecturally of all. We knew fairly early on what we were going to do with it. Previously, most of it had been painted – lots of gold paint. The capitals were gold as well

as the plasterwork under the tablets. Every time we tried enrichment it just did not work – looked completely wrong. If ever there was a house where I wanted the architecture to stand out, it is here. It seemed that the simpler it was, the better it looked.'

The simplicity of his solutions was, however, typically deceptive. The banished gold was replaced by subtly different whites, modulating the architectural forms in direct sympathy with the reasoning that shaped them. It is a contradiction of all restoration that, whilst searching for the spirit of the original, inevitably it bears the mark and spirit of current taste. Even as we peel away the face of the nineteenth century from an eighteenth-century house, we re-make it in the image of our own preoccupations, like actors re-interpreting a role. The architecture of Beningbrough is undeniably theatrical, like David Mlinaric's illusory paint. It is a set for our imaginations to wander in, now peopled by the National Portrait Gallery with Whigs and vanished beauties of eighteenth-century society. Its stylish arrangements of bare furniture, sometimes of operatic grandeur, like the crimson bed in the style of Marot that swoops in the state bedchamber, point towards a taste as contemporary to us as it was to its original inhabitants, the Bourchiers.

Above left: The entrance front of Beningbrough looking across the courtyard from the clock tower arch to the bell tower.

Above right: The staircase hall left fittingly bare except for one marble bust, and William Thornton's cantilevered wood staircase, a sculpture in its own right.

Right: The hall, two storeys high and an impressive example of English Baroque. The dwarfed figure of David Mlinaric, who restored Beningbrough, gives an idea of the scale. Deceptively painted many subtle shades of white, the monochromatic effect reveals the architecture. The only furniture is a set of early eighteenth-century painted hall chairs.

Above: The closet, beside the main bedroom, was used as a washing-
and dressing-room as well as a snug place to sit during cold winters.
The arrangement of tiered blue and white pots and plates is a Dutch
idea brought to England in the early eighteenth century by Daniel
Marot, architect to William of Orange. The tapestry wing armchair
is also eighteenth century as is the engraving on the easel.

Right: The state bedroom on the ground floor. It was the usual
practice in large houses of the seventeenth and eighteenth centuries to
have all the main rooms, including the bedrooms, interconnected. The
bed is dressed in crimson damask with the carved and damask-covered
canopy copying the carved cornices made by Thornton and his team
of Yorkshire craftsmen.

DAVID MLINARIC

Working at Home in Chelsea
Medieval House in Suffolk

David Mlinaric is well known for his historical accuracy. Decoration is a matter of biography for him; like someone writing about a person, only his heroine is a house where he goes back to all the sources and patches together what the truth might have been, then reconstructing it after his own fashion. Often there will be gaps that intuition must fill.

In his place of work in London, his talents have been called upon to make an autobiography, a self-portrait of the kind of place he wanted to live and work in. When he was re-decorating the Assembly Rooms in Bath, he found a reference in a contemporary letter to the fact that the walls and ceilings of a particular room were painted yellow and blue. It was up to him to decide exactly which hue would do. In London he has shared the billing with the house, taking cues from what he found there. The bannisters for the staircase and gallery in the main studio were copied from one found there. The past mingled with the present is a potent adviser in matters of colour too. In the corridor, downstairs, when the walls were stripped, a marvellously atmospheric mottled pink and green of old plaster and scraps of peeling paint was revealed. With a bit of handiwork on areas that were not so pleasing to match them up, a romantic finish of elegant decay was achieved, half a lie, but a lie that tells the truth about the past of the house, a studio belonging to generations of Chelsea artists since the nineteenth century, whilst at the same time fitting in with his own preoccupations about the mood of a place, its *genius loci*.

Above: David Mlinaric in his London house. On the table beside him a Victorian pincushion and mugs of sharp pencils. Simple objects such as these which have no particular value except the virtue of being pleasingly functional give meaning to a place. Behind them a black vase lamp and a basket of camellias.

Right: A room as much for working in as relaxing achieved by using good furniture instead of office desks. When choosing colours for chairs there is often no need to keep to one colour pattern. David Mlinaric uses green, red, brown and a rich yellow, all from the same strong colour family, echoing the Turkish carpet, and the deep green paint of the fireplace. The gasolier, the wild arrangement of evergreens, the miniature ladder, postcards and reference books mix business with pleasure.

His work is all about his understanding of life and so it is natural that the two should meet in this building. It is neither quite an office nor absolutely a house. Instead of functional and perversely ugly office furniture, he prefers to surround himself with good-looking antiques, whilst there are always the necessities of work, spaces to unroll plans, to sit in conference, to draw and research, close to the comfortable sofas.

'Restoration', said David Mlinaric, 'should not preclude the inclusion of new things.' However, he is lucky to be able to rely on his instinct to supply the right answer as readily as the available facts. He knows this by now, and this gives him the confidence that anybody needs to make decisions about how a room ought to be. 'It is interesting to see that scientific research upon the ageing of pigments comes up with many of the same results as my informed guesses as to the original colour.' He deserves his own compliment. In appearance elegantly attenuated like a new portrait of Aubrey Beardsley, he is the very portrait of his own place of work and living in London: various, calm, thoughtful, sure, unfussy. A combination of artist and academic in particular proportion.

Left: A corridor becomes rather more than you might expect in a small house under David Mlinaric's eye. The end becomes a focal point. A very formal marble urn and column-shaped cupboard, bare plastered walls with scraps of the paint that happened to be beneath old wall-paper, romantically suggest faded grandeur, an idea taken up in the architectural prints of old buildings.

Above left: In a bedroom completely hung with patterned fabric taken from an old document the curtains and bedcover fold rather than flounce keeping disciplined what could be over-powering.

Above right: A small sitting-room, reminiscent of a Victorian railway carriage, with a day-bed which converts it into a bedroom or 'couchette' at night.

Standing alone in miles of cornfield, its roofs and red brick chimneys rising over the great oaks and a broad wash of sky overhead, is a house that David Mlinaric chose for himself in the country, restoring it to its proper family place and sixteenth-century simplicities. The atmosphere is 'very Dutch, very calm and chaste', the country flat East Anglia on the Norfolk/Suffolk borders where the weather, when it's dry, is dry indeed, all wind and sun, and the seasons change from bleak to wild green and pale straw gold. Inside the house he abides by his golden rule, 'Are things suitable, not merely effective?' Much of the work involved re-instating the architect's original intentions: leading on windows was copied and replaced, fancy bathrooms and kitchen rejected; instead, radiators, sinks, door knobs, hinges, bricks for the hearth and a plain white bath from the builder's yard plus taps were bought locally. Things from elsewhere were allowed when they had the necessary simplicity and sympathy – a French carved wooden basin with brass taps, now in the attic bathroom. The radiators are visible; covering them up 'cuts down the heat, and you can disguise them anyway by painting them to blend with the walls.' Generations of farmers had lived here, finally sealing off the top floor and dividing the ground floor into boxes. 'Now it is four rooms again, all with their original hair plaster walls, the upstairs washed cool blue or green, the only coloured rooms in the house. The three doors of this floor were found in the roof made into a pigeon coop and covered with dead pigeons. I sensed they would fit and they did.' The result of this weaving in of every strand that he could find to do with the past of the house is that satisfactory feeling of 'rightness', so hard to pin down, 'the feeling that one should have a bit of respect for one's surroundings, there are the magic aspects of places which should be considered'.

Above: Thorpe Hall feels older than it looks and it looks sixteenth century. A country house for David Mlinaric, Dutch in flavour with a touch of Gothic, the windows face each other, the light flows through.

Right: The entrance hall, with its Gothic door, brick floor and wrought iron treelight with night light cups – an image repeated in the oil painting above the hall table – has an atmosphere typically Mlinaric.

44

Left: The drawing-room, the calm of the architecture respected, and reflected in the choice of things. On the floor local Norfolk rush matting, the pattern of which is repeated in miniature in herringbone weave cloth on the chairs and in the flame pattern curtains; by the fire an Oriental rug. Over it a view of the Capability Brown landscape at Redgrave. A room where books find themselves in steady piles, where the white-shaded lamps are capped to throw their light downwards so keeping the room pleasantly dim.

Top: An attic bedroom – 'it looks like an upside down ship' – has blue wash walls, as cold and as soft as you can get. No frills; the house demands the dignity of cleanlined furniture such as the chair by the dressing-table and the painted garden seat by the patchwork cover, which in turn relates to a screen covered in a collage of eighteenth-century prints, wallpapers and fragments.

Above: The attic bathroom with French wooden basin and brass taps, the rest of the furniture plain wooden. Garden flowers and lavender scent the room.

47

TOM PARR

Rooms in Eaton Square

When asked to define good taste, Elsie Mendl replied, 'Suitability, suitability, suitability . . .' These words would suit Tom Parr, a director of the notable and respected firm of Colefax & Fowler who have defined the 'English country house' look, mostly because they have designed for hundreds of English country houses. Obviously his work for other people must be made to suit their tastes, although they may sometimes be persuaded to adjust their ideas to what he sees as a more convenient solution. 'Some like to go into the minutest details, others go glazed at the mention of a door handle. But if someone says, "I don't care, just make me a room," it can be an absolute nightmare. I like people to take an interest, even to argue.' His only rule is that rooms should be both literally and atmos-pherically comfortable for the people who are going to use them. Convention matters not at all in the face of priorities – your needs might dictate that the largest room in your house should become the kitchen, complete with dog basket, television and all the paraphernalia of modern living.

Tom Parr's own home is a case in point. Two large rooms are divided by double doors which open up during the day to make one enormous bed-sitting room. 'The whole point of the room is that it is a muddle, but it is a muddle that works, for the rooms have changed little over twenty years.' In the sitting-room the handmade wallpaper in maroon and grey takes its pattern from an old damask; the carpet, called Rock Savage, is copied from the original at

Above: Tom Parr in his dining-room and guest-room. Behind him is the velvet sofa which doubles as a bed, above it one of the Indian Raj paintings from the Impey Collection.

Right: The dining-room has the atmosphere of a library with fake bird's eye maple bookcases and shaded reading lights. The Indian Raj paintings, subdued colours and collection of Imari-ware pots suggest the style of the early nineteenth century. The dining-table is a Colefax design and can be extended to seat six people.

Cholmondeley Castle. Chairs in yellow and green brocade and pink and yellow cotton face donkey-grey and dark brown sofas. The best piece in the room, a signed stool, is the jealously guarded province of Basil, the spaniel. Books pile up, paintings are decorative views of Claremont's gardens, a house and park recently restored by the National Trust. In the bedroom tomato cotton-weave walls, book-lined, are hung with paintings, including a delicious William Nicholson of Marie Tempest at a costume fitting, and the bed, a Colefax design, converts into a huge sofa in the daytime. Cupboards and bathroom are concealed on either side of the window and through them a passage leads to the dining-room, where guests can sleep as well as eat, on another sofa-bed. But the mood here is personal, not for reproduction in clients' homes: 'A house is not an advertisement for Tom Parr, it's for the owners. When you walk into a room, you should think "What a lovely atmosphere" and not just notice individual objects, because a true designer is a receptacle for peoples' dreams. It is his job to realise them.'

Left: The drawing-room, composed of two major rooms divided by double-doors with the far room becoming a bedroom when the green velvet Colefax-designed sofa turns into a bed. The best piece of furniture is the red velvet stool reserved for Basil, the spaniel. Outsized patterns are used for the wallpaper, hand made from an old damask design, and the carpet, 'Rock Savage', is also a copy. The cornice and architraves are marbled. In the far room a wardrobe and bathroom are concealed behind panels on either side of the window. Reflected in the pier glass is one of a set of six paintings of the Claremont Gardens.

Above: Through the double-doors the walls are covered with a tomato red cotton-weave but the curtains and carpet are the same in both rooms creating one scheme when the doors are open.

51

NICHOLAS HASLAM

A Hunting Lodge in Hampshire

Pevsner, in his Hampshire volume of *The Buildings of England* describes the house thus: 'Georgian but with a pretended Jacobean front, i.e., three gables, the middle one higher, shaped, with steep ogee top carrying urns. Nothing behind the gables. In front of the house a lake.' The date of the house, around 1740, means that it is a bit of an architectural anachronism, deliberately so, a survival rather than a revival. It was planned to be seen rather than to be seen in, and from a distance, when it was the fashion to see curious buildings from the windows of great houses. The great house was Dogmersfield Park, but the cottage was not easily visible from it, rather it was a folly beyond the others that the Mildmays who lived there had built for them. It was better seen from the top of a belvedere, which, along with a triumphal arch, a Palladian Bridge and

statuary, satisfied the fashionable tastes of the family. But not for long. Scarcely a hundred years later all else was gone, as the landscape movement, in the hands of Capability Brown, swept all before it. The hunting lodge (King John's or Henry's according to taste and preference) escaped, a home for gamekeepers, in the remnants of the royal hunting grounds that covered most of Hampshire. John Fowler discovered the lodge after the last war and left it to the National Trust. The idea of follies has always appealed to the great interior decorators; their mixture of caprice and their games with grandeur. They are houses playing at being houses. Nicholas Haslam, who lives there now, has maintained the style of John Fowler inside the house. Fowler's world remains intact outside, the pleached hornbeams, the geometric plan of the garden with its

Above: Nicholas Haslam in his London showroom.

Right: View of the hunting lodge from the lake. The gates have been specially designed to echo the architecture and the lawn is flanked by giant pleached hornbeams. The garden itself is divided into a series of 'rooms'.

'rooms', divided from one another by hedges and surrounded by lake and woods. The garden room preserves that mood of cool English elegance that owes its calm to quite a lot of off-white paint, pale marbled door surrounds, dove grey and sands, bleached boards covered with coir mats with rugs spread over them, and marvellous carnation chintz on sociable, facing sofas. A huge glass vase of untidy sprays admits a pleasing disorder into the room, as well as individual flowers of particular beauty in rough jugs and pots. The drawing-room with pink-washed distemper walls opens onto the terrace. Distemper has a softness of colour, something to do with the way that it reflects light, which is not reproducible in other paints. In the dining-room the walls are painted with false panels and hung with prints of Michelangelo's gateways in Rome.

Left: The garden-room, built at the far end of the garden to catch the view of the lake. It burgeons with flowers and has an operational potting shed beyond. Though a garden-room it is furnished as a drawing-room, with twin sofas covered in a glazed carnation chintz and a Turkey-carpet padded seat between them, facing a Gothic two-seater.

Above: The dining-room, long and narrow with Gothic windows echoed in the cut of the pelmets. The severity of the high back leather chairs is softened by the circular table dressed with a full-length cloth. Pink roses in the window, Wellington on a column on the table.

GEOFFREY BENNISON

By the Sea at Brighton

Geoffrey Bennison's interiors are massed with objects, a menagerie of shapes, with tribes of furniture as various as the ark. An immense camel reflects upon its bronze face in a mirror, sitting on a chest of drawers. Busts, surrounded with coral branches and old books, turn in amazement on a great wardrobe; a giraffe stands on his London desk, a covey of small pictures flies in formation over the door. Such groups are at the heart of his work, pattern on pattern on pattern, bronze beyond bronze.

He has his rules, though, and this order was not achieved through chaos of any kind. In his own words, the golden rule is 'something mad on top of something very good, or something very good on top of something mad'. In Brighton, where his taste for rich dark colour has been lightened by the sea, the mad and the very good are interchangeable. Marble lions on a marble fireplace part-obscure the Indian picture that sits behind them, rather than being formally hung. The point here lies in contrast,

Above: Geoffrey Bennison in his Brighton apartment, where areas of interest are created by weight of colour. Just such is the table covered with an old embroidery and laden with blue and white pots.

Right: The drawing-room: the walls are neutral to offset so many colours and textures. Textiles are loosely thrown over sofas and chairs, arranged to show the latter's shapes and sometimes revealing the legs. Outsize objects such as the stone lions on the chimney piece, the giant blue and gold pots and the ceiling-high lacquer screen are a particularly Bennison touch.

56

between cold stoniness and old colour, not in holy admiration of things for themselves. He will often show only the bit he likes best. If a covered chair has interesting carving he will 'let it show its legs', but he will tend to hide more than half of almost everything, producing rooms rich in mysteries.

'It was all very haphazard,' said Bennison of his early days as an antique dealer and decorator, 'but it jelled as time went on.' A student at the Slade in the early forties, a good painter, 'but not good enough for me', he spent years in Switzerland, and on returning to London found his bank manager saying, 'Do you realise that financially you are on the floor?' So he gathered up some of the things he had collected over the years, sold them, and that is more or less how it started. He has always chosen not only for quality but also for effect, and has a way of seeing objects as beautiful before other people: cheap embroideries, simple geometry on Moroccan rugs and the pleasing clash of pattern were added to the canon of classic interior design largely

through his efforts. He has always introduced an air of temporariness to his interiors, as if things have been allowed to stop *en route* to another destination, and have chosen the happiest of places to catch their breath. A red length of fabric will lie over the sour red of an upholstery, books will not be serried, a picture may hang in front of them as if awaiting judgement from a connoisseur, and yet the balance of final arrangement will be there.

He has kept a painter's eye for colour, mixing up paint in ways which people have never quite seen before. He can spend months working on sketches and water-colours to present to a client and this might be the extent of the job; some just take over from there. The Brighton flat is a sampler of Bennisonisms. Screens covered with wild designs conceal dull corners and break up unwanted architectural lines. But it is the comfort of his rooms that has taken priority. Nothing is less likely in one of his interiors than a delight to the eye that turns out to be a jolt to the system.

Below: The far end of the drawing-room arranged in two ways. Left: The area is patterned with Bokhara needlework table covers, a Louis XVI fauteuil, a Conran basket chair cushioned with Broderie de Tetuan, and a Kelim on the floor. The overall effect is dominated, but not overpowered, by the vast Levy-Dhurmer painting. Right: The same tables are used, but uncovered. Here objects tell a quieter story: a shimmering mother-of-pearl chest, a wooden unicorn, seventeenth- and eighteenth-century Chinese blue and white porcelain and a shell from Morocco.

Right: In the Brighton bedroom the bed is covered in antique, gold-appliqued bois de rose silk, the carpet is art nouveau, the screen is Spanish embossed leather, the chair in front, Queen Anne. Lighting is subdued. Leather-bound books take their place as an integral part of the decoration. Plain velvet on the armchair relieves the many patterns.

BERNARD NEVILL
The Victorian Manner in Chelsea

Bernard Nevill has a mind that brims with detail, a bale of patterned twists and scraps from the decorative arts, his warehouse of reference. He is stitched firmly into the life of design in this country. After studying at St Martin's and the Royal College of Art in the mid-fifties he taught fashion, textile and theatre design and book illustration before becoming the genius behind Liberty prints. In recent years he has worked principally for the colour-mad Italians, and has made an eccentric hiding place for himself in Chelsea. West House has proved to be a spiritual home. Designed by Philip Webb for the water-colourist George Price Boyce, friend and chronicler of the Pre-Raphaelite Brotherhood, it was the first house of its kind built for an artist to live and work in. Date, 1869, site, a corner of the Chelsea rectory grounds with kindred activity close by – Carlyle's house within sight, Rossetti at the Queen's House, William de Morgan's pottery a few yards south. Bernard Nevill had lived in Chelsea for many years when, needing momentary refuge between houses, he was offered the remaining lease on West House. He moved in for six months and, despite looming impracticalities, was gradually beguiled – by the associations, the architecture, 'the fortress-like feeling of privacy', the quiet and the views of the 300-year-old mulberry tree, fig and vine planted by Boyce, blue and pink bluebells in spring in the small wood of the rectory gardens where Charles Kingsley wrote *The Water Babies*. Later Fate moved the church commissioners to sell him the freehold. His intense and knowledgeable care has returned West House to its original atmosphere, or rather to that of Boyce and Webb crossed with the virtues of an old-fashioned well-run country house. This is his forte. 'I have a nostalgic weakness for all the domestic trivia formerly associated with large country houses – the enamel and brass

Above: Bernard Nevill in West House.

Right: The drawing-room, a tumble of cushions on a worn leather Chesterfield, a Ziegler carpet and piles of books where the only sounds are the crackling of logs on the fire and the ticking of a clock. The outsize gramophone is used by Mr Nevill to amplify his collection of old 78s. William Morris curtains hang on wooden poles. Everything here has lived at least one life before.

watering cans, the embroidered "hot water" covers, butlers' aprons, Kent's knife-cleaning machines, pottery "improved" bread crocks, pickling jars, coal scuttles *et al*.' He has always preferred the slightly shabby and faded look of old 'unmodernised' country houses to the more popular school of new white paint and coloured walls: a reflection of his upbringing in Devon, cared for by three Edwardian great-aunts, with his Uncle George's reminiscences of walking tours with Tennyson and scouting with Baden-Powell, his Aunt Nancy's amateur theatricals and fruit *compotes* with Devonshire cream – part of a delicious vegetarian diet to which he is still faithful. ('Stomachs are not cemeteries' said the aunts.) Other tastes were, and are, for the then unfashionable Victorians, for the Arts and Crafts movement, for the arts of 1900 to 1930, for old periodicals – he has Queen Alexandra's monogrammed copies of *The Graphic*. As a student he became close friends with the famous Titian-haired Marchesa Casati whom his Aunt Nancy had known in the Marchesa's heyday in Rome. She introduced him to the arts of her time and the impeccable pages of the *Gazette du Bon Ton*. His information is partly visual but he gathers in everything pertinent to a given moment. Music, too, is a great influence and love, strongly allied to his sense of colour: 'While colouring a collection of designs I am constantly hearing and listening to the notes of colours – sounding them out, arranging

Above: The Edwardian tiled basement kitchen with a spread of nursery food in the background, old kitchen appliances, like a Kent Knife polisher, and Gimson ladder-back chairs.

Right: The dining-room with billiard table lights. On the far wall a giant painting, Gascoyne's 'Turning the Plough', wine cooler filled with larkspurs, mahogany table and chairs from a Scottish boardroom.

them into deliberate discords, dissonances or harmonies in the same manner as a composer which, given the gift, I would ideally like to be.' West House is a monument to his salvages from the heartless demolition of the past thirty years. With five floors, from traditionally tiled kitchens, breakfast-room/servants hall re-painted British below-stairs bottle green to the attics, it is large enough to accommodate such greater and lesser pieces as Henry Whitaker's bookcases from the old Conservative Club library in the drawing-room, the massive Gothic oak-framed armorial stained glass wall-screen from Norfolk House, plush from Mentmore, William Morris hand-woven and blocked fabrics, boardroom table and chairs from the Prudential, trellis from the Norman Shaw house in Queen's Gate. It is his greatest pleasure to track down the rare and obscure for his friends and for himself, to add to the mellowed layers of this amazing house where the atmosphere is truly complete if the place is humming with industry other than its own – when brass and mahogany gleam and there is a smell of beeswax and baking, of log fires and larders stocked with all the nursery food he loves.

Left: The guest bedroom. Half-tester hung with nineteenth-century lace, window seat with Victorian grospoint cushions, all furniture in satinwood, the art nouveau card table inlaid with tulipwood, carrying a single specimen vase and boxes covered in original nineteenth-century chintzes.

Above: The bed hung with Mentmore red plush, back panel of seventeenth-century appliqued velvet, bedcover of seventeenth-century embroidered silk strapwork, 1860s grospoint carpet, Slingsby library ladder.

CHARLES BERESFORD-CLARK
A Georgian Fishing Lodge in Suffolk

In the mid-eighteenth century Sir Izaak Walton's sport had become the latest catch of fashion, and some humble fishing lodges shook themselves and became Architecture. This one, in a landscape hiding from Constable in Suffolk, seems to have been built for the delight of those rustling fashionable guests, angling for one another as much as for trout.

Over the years it has shown some of its secrets to its owner Charles Beresford-Clark. It is no haphazard flung-up affair, but rather 'would have been of the most intense interest, giving someone who had been on the Grand Tour a chance to test his own taste and that of his architect'. It was first rediscovered by David Hicks twenty or so years ago. He planted fine hornbeam hedges that flank the house like the wings of a stage-set, and had Sir Raymond Erith design the *oeil-de-boeuf* window into the dark kitchen. By the time Charles Beresford-Clark came along, the house had subsided into wildness again. He swept the dust away with a marvellous bright eye for colour.

It is essentially a one-room house. There is an undercroft of a kitchen, the wings hold a staircase and small, small bedroom, but the 'saloon' is what it is all so beautifully about. From its grace and airily novel proportions many would guess it to be the work of Sir John Soane who re-modelled the main house on the estate in 1796, but Charles Beresford-Clark ascribes it to Sir Robert Taylor on account of its resemblance to Taylor's *Asgill* house in Richmond. The fine proportions of the façade go slightly and endearingly wrong at the sides, but inside is another matter. The door is deliberately low to increase the effect of the height as you enter the room, and the fireplace is off-centre. It looks central, but the architect must have judged its placing by instinct. The room is arranged simply, its main element the lovely Suffolk matting, which, with its natural associations and the plain unbleached calico opulence at the windows, provides a pleasing foil to the room's architectural formality.

Above left: The fishing lodge, circa 1750 and probably designed by Sir Robert Taylor.

Above right: Charles Beresford-Clark by the canal.

Right: The saloon of the fishing lodge has classic proportions and the plasterwork on the ceiling depicts the four seasons. Beresford-Clark deliberately tried to let the beauty of the architecture speak. On the floor he uses Suffolk rush matting, the window blinds are of plain unbleached calico decked out with striped rosettes, the chandelier is carved wood and lit with wax candles, there is a comfortable armchair, a striped ottoman and a Pugin oak table.

LAURA ASHLEY

A Farmhouse in Wales
Château in Northern France

Laura Ashley is a number of people. She and her husband Bernard, he mechanical, she artistical, started it all with tea-towels printed on the kitchen table. Now her family and her family-spirited workforce go on famously. The name is more appropriate than any made-up one could be, and that is the mainspring of her extraordinary success, that her ideas fitted the times like a glove and her clothes fitted the ideas of how millions of people all over the world wanted to look. She has always said that all she did was to make what she wanted for herself available to other people. Each collection is an aspect of the same idea, a retreat into a softer focus, the gentleness of an old photograph, a chemical-free, clean place, picked from the past as a solution to present stress. Her places of retreat in Wales and France are characteristically close to the Front whilst seeming to be miles from it. The château at Remaisnil in the Somme was a direct swap for a terraced house in Chelsea and with the help of a few small planes and a local airport the Ashleys commute. The reason for the choice of the château and of the Welsh house was the same, convenience given business considerations, and it works. The Ashleys have always combined family with work and work with life.

At her two houses the ideas for new papers and fabrics are tried out on the family first; in recent collections they have

Above: Laura Ashley at home in Wales. The conservatory, a recent addition, is being filled with palms and statues in the Victorian manner.

Right: The drawing-room, decorated in high Victorian taste with Laura Ashley paper copied from a Harewood House original at Clifton Castle. The drape of the pelmet was copied from a nineteenth-century pattern book. In the background, the new conservatory.

been from increasingly responsible historical sources, copied from paintings, like the striped paper in a small bedroom at Remaisnil which Laura Ashley spotted in a painting by Louis Darcis, 'The Unforeseen Accident', 1801, in Mario Praz's marvellous book, *Interior Decoration*. The French manner at Remaisnil is tempered for the farmhouse in Wales, which is darker, huddled for warmth behind thick curtains, with a cosy mass of furniture and a lot of patterns. This time they are copies dug out from all sorts of odd places. The curtains in the drawing-room were copied from a piece discovered on the foot-board of a bed in Clifton Castle, whilst the dining-room wallpaper and curtains are from an original found behind some bookcases at Wythenshaw Hall. Here things glint in the gloom, glass domes and glass vases, crystal pendants and the glass eyes of birds. The success of Laura Ashley has always been as an editor rather than as a designer, the adaption of ideas rather than the creation of them. As time passes she is getting closer and closer to her sources, producing a revival of some of the classic patterns from her two favourite periods, late eighteenth-century France and Victorian England, for which Remaisnil and the Welsh farmhouse are the laboratories and showcases.

Left: The Blue bedroom, a small single room with the French Polonaise bed dressed in a textile design adapted from a Lyons woven silk. The wallpaper stripe is taken from one seen in a painting by Louis Darcis. The rest of the furniture is French.

Above: The eighteenth-century château at Remaisnil on the Somme and the French retreat of the Ashley family. It is decorated in the styles of Louis XV and XVI and uses a wide range of the Laura Ashley collection of papers and textiles.

71

A nostalgic and unconsciously arranged still life on a hall table.

THE PERSONAL VIEW

'Mrs Furnish at St. James's has ordered lots of fans and China, and India Pictures . . .'

T. Baker, *The Fine Lady's Airs*, 1707

As the heroine remarks in *Barefoot in the Park*, surveying her empty flat with a few old chairs standing about, 'the final style of the apartment will not emerge until the bride's own personality has been established'. The more we see of life, the more we may tend to want to be in a place amongst things that have seen a lot of it pass. Or like Picasso, we might choose to keep turning the key in the lock; to walk away and live almost as a visitor amongst things that have a life of their own. Picasso lived in many kinds of houses. Gertrude Stein tells a story of visiting him in his studio. 'Sit down,' said Picasso, but there were no chairs, so everyone just stood. Other people would come and Picasso would say 'sit down' to them too, and everyone would stand, quite comfortably for hours.

Some houses have been dealt out to the people who live there, like Chatsworth. They make considerable demands on their owners, and in return repay the anxiety and responsibility of great treasures constantly in need of care. But the point of all these houses is that their essential qualities cannot be bought. It is the people who have chosen them or who just find themselves living in them that make them beautiful, strange, important, special. Many of them are very private places, retreats from the world and its difficulties. Others are the bold gestures of personalities who are larger than life, and prove it by putting their dreams into houses, like Erté's château outside Paris, or Pierre Loti's extraordinary home at Rochefort. The best effects are seldom studied. Atmosphere collects as dust and things settle. Houses are like faces and they weather into character, but faces which have been incessantly restored can become characterless masks. As *Vogue* remarked in 1925 in an article called 'A Revolt against some kinds of Excellence', 'We shall Find Any Interior that Does not Flow from Our Own Instincts a Cold Unconvincing Background for Ourselves.' Sometimes looking at other people's houses can make our own seem hopeless cases. Such order, such peace, such easiness. The carpet is always greener on the other side of the wall. In the end it is the haphazard, unconscious meeting of need with what is to hand that makes a room comfortable. There is a scene in Noël Coward's *Design for Living* which exactly puts us in the picture:

> *Grace:* Gilda has been showing me this perfectly glorious apartment.
>   Don't you think it's lovely?
> *Otto:* (looking around) Artistically too careful, but professionally superb.
> *Gilda:* (laughing lightly) Behave yourself, Otto!

Otto would find nothing to accuse in the houses on the following pages. They have not been arranged with other people in mind, or what they might think, or with more than a glance in the direction of fashion. Professional not at all, but personally superb.

For a long time, since the emergence of houses built to the glory of their owners, an effect of grandeur and power was the point. The idea that our homes should be our castles has remained with us, through the self-important villas of the Victorians and in our semis. But the treasures of a great house like Chatsworth, miraculous as they may be, are only part of the story. The secrets of these places do not lie in the rarity of the things inside them. No matter what, the point is seeing how people live there. In a small untidy place or in fine echoing halls, there is equal room in the imagination for both.

CHATSWORTH
Living with a Great House in Derbyshire

Chatsworth in Derbyshire was built by many hands, shaped by many minds, but it began, rising out of a bleak, wild country, in 1552. It gathered in magnificence through the lives of ten Dukes of Devonshire, enriched particularly by those in the eighteenth century, lying virtually dormant under others, until to the present Duke and Duchess Chatsworth became home, honour and time-consuming delight.

It is three hundred and sixty-five times bigger than the average house. There are one hundred and seventy-five rooms and twenty-one kitchens and workshops; as the Duchess has said, it is a terrible place to house-train a puppy, and a non-stop race against decay. 'I used to think you could arrange one of the big rooms upstairs, and that it could be frozen like a photograph, and that nothing need be changed as long as it was kept clean. I was wrong. Curtains, bed hangings, coverings on furniture, bindings (like the beasts from which they are made) must be fed, paintings on walls and ceilings restored, carpets mended if old and beautiful . . . it is like running to stand still.' But run they do, and the life of Chatsworth, in their own

Above: Chatsworth House, home of the Duke and Duchess of Devonshire, seen from the River Derwent.

Right: The 11th Duke of Devonshire in his sitting-room. 'Sitting-room not study because I sit here.' The walls are lined with books, the Duke's collection encroaching on those of previous dukes, two shelves laid bare for the newcomers. Above the cases inscriptions such as 'Thoughts that breathe and words that hum' or, about Milton, 'A Poet blind yet bold'. The decor remains grand, shabby and untouched. Books and periodicals pile up but there is order within the disorder, bound volumes of the 'Racing Calendar' dating back centuries neatly shelved as are the classics of Balzac, Dostoevsky, Turgenev, etc. to current biographies, Isherwood, Waugh, Huxley, all in correct library order. 'The number of things in this house which I did not know existed is very substantial.'

studies, sitting-rooms and bedrooms, goes on like a house within a house, in an encouraging and usual muddle, within the rigorous lockings and unlockings, rounds of night-watchmen and massive galleried halls of treasure.

'You lose things, but you never know what you may find. Once on a winter afternoon when it was getting dark, I journeyed to the last room of the East Attics to look for something. It is quite a trek to get there – down the Book Passage to the Batchelor Passage, up to the stone stairs, past the lamp cupboards, turn right and it is the third room on the right. I opened the door and stopped dead, amazed to see an old man sitting among piles of books reading under a strong lamp. I was so surprised I said something like "I'm so sorry to disturb you" and fled back the way I had come. I have no idea who he was or what he was doing, and for all I know he still may be there.'

Left: The Blue drawing-room. Faded silk brocade walls and gilded cornices, even the outer window frames are painted gold to catch the light, a notion copied from the Hermitage in Leningrad. The grandeur of the decoration is made comfortable by the white cotton-covered armchairs, the chintz-covered sofa and the friendly fur rug on top of the Aubusson carpet. Pots of plants from the greenhouse, in this instance an orange tree which repeats the fruit being picked in the Sargent portrait. Old paintings and modern portraits by Lucien Freud and photographs mixed together.

Above: Outside the Blue drawing-room fresh flowers and plants are brought in from the garden by Mr Hopkins, head gardener, for the Duke – an expert horticulturalist himself – to see.

Left: The Duchess's bedroom. The painted four-poster bed is dressed with strictly cut canopy and no curtains on the end posts so that the view through the facing window is left unobstructed. The print on the canopy is repeated on the valance with a large motif for the border. Favourite pieces of porcelain, Epstein drawings of the children and piles of books make it a very personal room.

Top: The Duke's bathroom, crammed with paintings, cartoons and photographs to dwell on while lying in the bath.

Above: A single guest room.

MADRESFIELD

Inspiration for Evelyn Waugh in Worcestershire

In 1944, writing to Lady Dorothy Lygon about his newest novel, Evelyn Waugh wrote, 'There's a house as it might be Mad, but it isn't really Mad.' The house, indeed a mad house, was Madresfield, the novel *Brideshead Revisited*. The Lygon family have lived at Madresfield in Worcestershire since the sixteenth century. The longevity of their stay gave the house its particular quality, as each personality, and they were many and brightly coloured, left the ghost of his or her taste in a new corridor, drawing-room, chapel, toy, portrait, or just in the haunting gloom of a bedroom or the golden afternoon of the library. It is intensely atmospheric and suggests a novel, perhaps a different one from Waugh's even, at every turn.

Madresfield, high Victorian medieval fantasy encrusted onto a 1546 moated house, was principally the work of Philip Charles Hardwick, who designed the classical book-ing hall at Euston and the Great Western Hotel at Paddington. He allowed his classical sense to exaggerate at Madresfield and made a place where a fashionable imagination could feel at home in 1875. The magic still works, but for rather different reasons. Madresfield, cut off inside its moat, seems an island of a kind of English life as irrevocably past as medieval England.

The Arts and Crafts movement, along with the Folksong Revival, flourished in this part of the West Country. Its principal legacy at Madresfield is the extraordinary chapel, made from two bedrooms in 1865 but not decorated in its entirety until 1923. Like the library with its carved bookshelves, where Adam and Eve stand amongst the branches of the tree of knowledge and its forbidden fruit, the chapel seems both sacred and profane, both a nostalgic lie and its own sort of truth. Are these beautiful bindings to be read,

Above: The courtyard, an enthusiastic Victorian idea of what medieval England ought to look like, by Philip Charles Hardwick, 1875, has a maze in mosaic.

Right: The great hall from the minstrel's gallery, with Tudor and Stuart portraits where threadbare banners hang from the hammerbeam roof.

these pews for a real congregation? Madresfield is an odd mixture of fact and fiction. Waugh wrote in *Brideshead* of an art nouveau chapel, 'elaborately re-furnished in the Art and Crafts style of the last decade of the nineteenth century. Angels in printed cotton smocks, rambler roses . . .' Charles Ryder, Waugh's principal character, did not like it, sneering at, 'a beaten copper lamp of deplorable design . . . I think it's a remarkable example of its period. Probably in eighty years it will be greatly admired.'

Above: The staircase hall built by the 7th Earl Beauchamp in 1913 is remarkable for its great height and crystal balusters, inventive in the best Arts and Crafts manner of the time. Massive furniture and marble busts mingle with poignantly recent family portraits. The lions, bears and swans are the Lygon emblems.

Right: In the corner of a small gallery off the Long Corridor, a deserted rocking-horse. Madresfield is intensely atmospheric.

Overleaf: The Chinese bedroom, in the Victorian addition, has Neo-Oriental panelling of Chinese scenes in gold on black lacquer. The half-tester over the bed, is deeply draped with side curtains. The rose brocade sofa, although surprisingly large for a bedroom, looks right here. Not seen in the photograph is the cloud-painted ceiling and the fleur de lys and daisy carpet, a touch of William Morris. This is possibly the room that suggested the death scene of Lord Marchmain to Evelyn Waugh in 'Brideshead Revisited'.

PIERRE LOTI

A Writer's House in Rochefort

Julien Viaud was born in a prim little town called Roche-fort, near La Rochelle in Western France, in 1850. In time his imagination and frustration would lead him to become one of the most intensely romantic of writers, calling him-self Pierre Loti, adored by the most glamorous figures of *le Tout Paris*. But his strange life of travelling, hardship, luxury and loneliness, troops of friends and isolation of spirit, found their testament not only in a stream of volup-tuous travelogues and journeys through his heart, but also behind the unassuming façade of his family home, 141 Rue Saint-Pierre, now called Rue Pierre Loti.

Fleeing from the trauma and intensity of his early life, changes in the family fortunes that left the Viauds penni-less, the death of his hero, his handsome brother, Loti escaped from Rochefort to write a different life for himself on the blank sheet of the sea. His travels brought forth floods of words, biographical writings, that showed that his escapes in disguise, his life as a circus performer and as

Above: Pierre Loti's house in Rochefort, his home since childhood. The simple terraced façade gives no hint of the surprise within.

Right: The Red drawing-room where family prayers were said daily. Loti had it hung with red velvet to please his mother, the earlier drab brown painted walls still remain beneath it. The portrait is of Loti in Arabian dress and beyond it the curtained doorway leads to the Blue salon made for Loti's wife Blanche.

a sailor, were all attempts to find himself. He looked everywhere, in other men and women, and fell in love narcissis-
tically with anyone who seemed to hold the secret of who
he could be, his heroine Aziyade, or a wild-eyed Turk. It
was for this person that he searched by candlelight in
tombs and cellars past rows of mummies in Egypt,
amongst the exquisite women of Japan or the crew of the
ships he travelled on. The rooms he created at Rochefort,
contrived more and more intricately as the years passed by,
turned a simple, unassuming house into a Chinese puzzle
as elaborate as his personality. Rooms were conjured from
others, were superimposed, reached by outside stairways,
by plunging levels or hidden doors, or appeared to be
suspended where no room had been before.

The Japanese salon was followed by a Chinese pagoda,
while a salon, strictly Louis XVI, satisfied the conventional

*Above: Loti's childhood desk, nothing was changed, nothing was
ever thrown away. On top of the desk a china bear jar which his aunt
would fill with pralines for him.*

*Right: The salle de Momi where Loti used to work. The many
signed photographs are from crowned heads and celebrities such as
Queen Alexandra, Sarah Bernhardt, Annie Besant. In the closets
between the bookcases are scores of richly embroidered Chinese,
Indian and Turkish costumes.*

taste of his wife, Blanche, to whom he played husband between voyages and passions, and which opened into a monumental hall, part-Gothic, part-Renaissance which satisfied Loti's sense of grandeur. There was also a peasant interior holding Breton souvenirs, a bedroom like a spartan cabin aboard ship with a narrow bed, and, most bizarre of all, a complete mosque, transported from Damascus, complete with ostrich eggs and tassels, and re-built in the house and courtyard.

Saved from demolition by Loti (who was one of Europe's first avid conservationists) and helped to France by 'honest smugglers', the mosque took its exotic place next to the unchanged rooms of his childhood, the red parlour of evenings by the fire, the narrow yellow dining-room which opened onto the courtyard, the bedrooms of his mother and aunt Claire. It was as if by binding the truth about with all these fantasies of other lives he could merge the two impulses that tore at him, the desperate search for solace, the desperate need for escape. At Rochefort they move in and out of one another, from room to room, world to world, reality to reality. Loti, who hated the passing of time and longed for perpetual youth and passion, built a private world for himself where his past and his present life could triumph over the world outside, in which in his magnificent parties he could be adored and photographed, in whose narrow bed he could dream that life was real, before waking up and being unable to face the fact. 'I am not myself,' he said. He died a national hero, three warships accompanied his coffin from Rochefort to Orleron. The house sits undisturbed and unnoticed behind the town street, more or less forgotten, like the man who lived there.

Left: The vast Renaissance room next to the Blue salon was built by Loti and took up most of the courtyard. At the far end the stone staircase was built in false perspective to give the effect of a gentle sweep and length. It leads up to the mosque. By the carved stone fireplace are never-forgotten chairs of his childhood.

Above: The mosque which Loti brought over from Damascus was installed in the 1880s.

Above: In the corner of the bedroom a simple wash stand, above it a painting of the Arabian desert.

Right: Loti's bedroom, a stark, white cabin, bare boards and grey woodwork. Muslim, Christian and Buddhist symbols and figures for spiritual reflection take their place beside the weapons, crossed fencing foils above the bed, near his rifle and sword. In the foreground a cast of his hand rests on Turkish embroidery.

92

DUNCAN GRANT
Living at Charleston in Sussex

Vanessa Bell discovered it. In 1916, riding on a wartime bicycle through high Sussex hedges, she found Charleston. At the time Duncan Grant was conscientiously objecting on a fruit farm in Suffolk, but Charleston was to become more than just a home for two painters with modern ideas, full of the news coming over from France from the brushes of Matisse, Dérain, Braque and Picasso. It was the place where the spirit of the Bloomsbury group took the air more than anywhere else, where it felt most at home out of London. Affairs, arguments, books ranged over everything under the sun, whilst paint flowed as freely as talk, over walls, canvas, furniture, fabric and pots, a holiday from Bloomsbury logic; it was messy and marvellous.

Who might be sitting out there on the lawn after lunch? Virginia and Leonard Woolf, Vanessa and Clive Bell, Lytton Strachey, Roger Fry . . . the familiar list lulls like the drone of bees. Bloomsbury had the power to promote and protect itself, to decorate itself, and Duncan Grant was decorated by Roger Fry in the Hogarth Press series, 'Living Painters', run by Leonard and Virginia. He wrote in 1923, 'His naturalness gives him his singular charm of manner. But more than this, he has a peculiar happiness of disposition. Although in developing his means of expression Duncan Grant has been very much influenced by the great modern masters, his talent is peculiarly English.' It was English enough not to be great, and French enough not to be dull, concerned as it was, in his case more than Vanessa Bell's, with idea more than technique, a charge levelled against the later productions of Fry's Omega workshops which put the Charleston style of Grant on sale in a shop in Fitzroy Square.

Left: Duncan Grant's studio, every surface irresistibly painted, with an incongruous china cabinet. Postcards, cuttings, memorabilia everywhere. To the far right a pre-war Heals chair given to Vanessa Bell by Virginia Woolf, near it an electric fire of the same epoch.

Above: Duncan Grant at the age of 87 in the garden at Charleston.

95

With Fry's ability to turn Duncan's prodigal decorations into high-minded art politics, Charleston became a shrine to those who felt that these were the pictures that went with Bloomsbury's words, their illustrations. But Charleston itself wriggles out of definitions, as Duncan Grant wriggled out of painting pictures according to Fry's tenets in later years. Charleston belongs to him and Vanessa Bell, a work of many hands but an expression of a delightful, singular personality. Swimmers hurl spray over a wooden chest, goldfish, fruit, flowers, stencils, patterns, urns, statuesque nudes and angular athletes vie for the eye's delight and attention, on walls, floors, furniture and doors. Fry concluded, 'It is indeed greatly to be regretted that so rare a talent as Duncan Grant shows for all kinds of decorative design can find so little outlet in our modern life, particularly since it is difficult to (sic) him to find scope within the limits of the easel picture for his finest gifts.' He found it at Charleston.

Above: The bathroom, panels painted of course; over the wash basin, a gushing fountain.

Right: A Bloomsbury tea at Charleston. The table painted, the crockery made by Quentin Bell and decorated by Duncan Grant. The walls stencilled with a patchwork of paint. Notes unfussily pinned to the chimney piece.

KAFFE FASSETT

Patterns and Colours in North London

Kaffe Fassett, in paintings, textiles, tapestries and embroideries has knitted together a palette that is fresh on the eye. Matisse spoke of how he loved to cut with a pair of scissors straight into painted paper, sculpting pure colour that way. Kaffe Fassett weaves subtle patterns and textures, rich dappled variations of both, stitching, knitting colour and digging into the history of pattern for his inspiration.

In his rooms off a grey North London street, colour sits everywhere and in baskets. The hanks of wool are all of complex shades; purples full of gentian blue, browns drenched with venetian reds and mauves, pinks dusted with amber, all the colours of Persian rugs, the dark oxbloods; and other things, the bleached colours of age, in Kelims, trunkfuls of cloth, Chinese pots. And then there is another scale, of colour as fresh as new paint, icy blue-white and lilac, lemon yellow and sap green, a palette from the Impressionists but, once learned from them, made his own.

Kaffe Fassett, painter, textile and knitting designer, in his London studio. Everywhere, reference points for his design work. Nothing costs more than a few pounds, bargains at market stalls, autumn leaves, grasses, lichen-covered stones, shells all have their particular beauty which he in turn uses in his knitting, paintings and tapestries. The wicker seat on the right of the picture is covered with a design of his, more are pinned to the wall. The window is shaded with an old Kashmir shawl. The contents of the room are an object lesson in his highly personal colour and design sense.

99

He can teach us the art of getting a lot from a little; seeing two colours side by side in an old costume, or the different whites of china against one another is his source for new work; in painting, where he represents the crowds of his influence, the troops of pots and weaves, and in his designs for embroidery and clothes. His home is not a living space so much as a workshop, where he and colour work together. It is not really decorated at all, it is the feeling of the place that gives that impression. A shawl hangs at the window for a curtain, furniture is really fabric notes for his own designs, it is a place decorated with ideas. Kaffe Fassett shows that once colour has set your imagination going, a room needs little else in it to be comfortable, just a few soft places to sit and a steady place to work.

Above: Ingredients for a still life in cold storage. A dresser used as an artist's palette with postcards, egg shells, tiles chosen for their special colour and patterns.

Right: A Kaffe Fassett still life in the background; in the foreground the real-life ingredients for another show how he crowds different ideas together into a new pattern.

RODERICK CAMERON
A Stone House in Provence

Roderick Cameron's house in Provence is an exactly realised scheme of build-ing and decoration. A ruin of pale stone was re-built to fit around the things to go inside it. An exercise in taste rare in its completeness, from the first he knew exactly what he wanted. The result has a serenity only found where form follows function and the spirit of place matches the temperament of the person who lives there. It was love at first sight. 'To reach it we had to bump along a gravel road, then down through some vines to a small derelict farm adjacent to a ruin. A date roughly carved over one of the doorways proclaimed the ruin to be early eighteenth century. It had no pretence to grandeur but great charm. Scrambling over half-fallen walls and peering through broken arches my imagination started working; here the kitchen; there the drawing-room and what a good place for the bedroom. The bait was taken. This was it. Excitement and plans. Fortunately Alexandre Favre, the house's architect, was there with his far more measured approach. It would be impossible to use any of the original foundations and certainly not any of the walls. The ruin would have to be razed completely but, as Favre pointed out, we had a gold mine in building material; a mass of tawny coloured stone that could be redressed. Still more important, it made things considerably easier to obtain a building permit if a building of some kind already existed. Furthermore the farmhouse could be turned into quiet rooms in which we could live while the rest was being finished. But of all the advantages what really won me over was the situation. The ruin terraced down amongst a wood of oak trees and faced due south overlooking fold after fold of gentle, forested hills in a view that was furnished in the middle distance by a little walled village which stood silhou-etted against some mountains.

Above: Roderick Cameron in his garden.

Right: The weather is mild enough to have a permanent stone table, and pale weathered chairs of subtle colour, naturally at home out of doors.

Left: The entrance hall, plate glass windows cleverly recessed to give maximum light and minimum glare. The muted colours of stone and marble, cool and elegant, in the spirit of the Greek and Roman sculptures.

Top: The shell-like staircase, a particularly modern curve, sweeps down from the hall to the dining- and drawing-room.

Above: View from the stairs towards the library passage. Here plate glass windows face the bookcases protected from sunlight by a loggia which runs outside.

Every time I visited the site the light was different; at times smudged with a heat haze of late summer and at others having every outline clean cut like etching a glass by the mistral. The boring mechanics over, we set to with the construction. The main part of the house was to be in the building tradition of the country; dry stone walls and Roman tiles for the roofs. The only real innovations were to be the plate glass windows which, along with the shutters, were to slide into the thickness of the walls. Large openings are frowned upon in this country of sun, but I find light all-important in a room, and this Favre achieved by running a loggia along the outside walls skirting the drawing-room. The questions of proportion were dictated by the size of the paintings and the different possessions I had been brought up with. There was to be nothing new in the house. I have never had any problems about colours and prefer them muted; the silver-green of the back of an olive leaf for the big room with off-white curtains, and beige for the hall and the shell-like stairs that curve down into the house. White or off-white, a faded mustard yellow, moss green and the soft blues of porcelain seem to be the dominant colours. As to materials, I like small patterned things, if patterned at all, and very often just colour on colour, the motive being barely discernible.'

Above: A guest bedroom with mirrored chest of drawers and skirted dressing-table, the prettiness of the room disciplined by formal trellis-patterned wallpaper.

Right: In the drawing-room where the proportions of the new building were dictated by the size of family portraits and possessions, off-white curtains drift in the breeze. The large portrait is of Lady Kenmare, Roderick Cameron's mother; below, Waterford glass.

MANOLO BLAHNIK
Three Rooms in Notting Hill

Manolo Blahnik was born in a white house, trellised and surrounded with bright banana trees in the Canary Islands. He came to England by a slow inclination, an increasing curiosity, more or less circumstance and the intervention of the two principal agents in his life, fate and friends. In a sense he could have lived anywhere and nowhere. His temperament, a real love of beauty for its own sake, and an awareness of its implications in everything, belongs to a world within a world and is interested in national frontiers only when they produce different cultural effects. These effects appear brilliantly in his shoe designs. Manolo Blahnik is one of the few people to make shoes more than they really ought to be; buzzing with historical associations, a drama for feet, at the least a delight-ful pair of creatures, at best shoes with souls. 'I feel very privileged to be part of this generation. I think we are the last people to understand what the style of life was before. I'm not unhappy now, because I have my own environment and couldn't care less about the rest.' His own environment is a huge cultural scrapbook. His shoes and the rooms he has lived in are pages from it: the paintings of Boldini with their glamour of white paint and mauve, their flick of the brush, the lightning lines of an evening shoe, 'Mary Queen of Scots always had boots under her dresses,' Pompeiian red, Catherine the Great, St Petersburg, Bird's-eye maple furniture, shoes all the colours of a king-fisher, a pair of slippers as if tossed from a bed in Versailles. He keeps a photograph album of glances; light switches,

Above: On a table top, flowers are just bunched in a vase; unarranged, they speak for themselves.

Right: Manolo Blahnik, shoe designer, in his pale pink sitting-room, drifts of longer than necessary curtains, with larger than life stone Roman bust on the floor. Formal seigneurial style with the odd twist that debunks.

Spanish shop windows, perfect façades; and of his rooms in other guises, severe with Venetian blinds and sofas covered in strict white canvas, or the turn of a head in a French nineteenth-century portrait. Preferences and passions are all mixed together, bows, drapes, flowers, Visconti, close friends who are loyal, shoe-crazed. He has imagined a possible present for the things he loves about the past and put it into shoes. When they are worn his conviction is passed on to those who wear them; a truly glamorous effect. His rooms are the same, his effects are unstriven for, happen like a quick smile. An enormous bust rests its chin on the arm of a small sofa, fabric is tacked up in great translucent drapes in an operatic fashion. His own shoes, handmade and understated (foreign shoes for men are vulgar he says, 'Only English shoes are possible for men'), star in the bedroom in rows, beside a huge wardrobe that irresistibly suggests packing for some long journey by train.

Above: Details of the dressing-room which is also a second bedroom. The Empire bed, fitted with day covers of piped blue ticking.

Right: The dressing-room. The wardrobe overflowing so neatly, battalions of shoes lined up in classes, wax candles, the curtains fine linen sheets just turned over and caught with a stitch and a ring to hang from a narrow brass rod.

Despite this refinement and his perfect manners, he is not tediously exquisite. There are plenty of normal things about, notes, television, bits and pieces jostle in unaffected, casual mixtures, there as much to remind as for themselves. The rooms are those of someone who lives successfully in the present by choosing from the past, this cast of satyrs, carved beds, chandeliers with burning candles. There is a poignancy in these things, the remnants of a beauty, like the shoes that remain after the dancers who whirled in them have vanished under the hill.

Right: The bedroom, antique bed from Christopher Gibbs, crisp good linen bedclothes. Colefax & Fowler chintz curtains, hung simply. A formal frieze below the cornice frames the room.

FELIX HOPE-NICHOLSON
A Family House in Chelsea

More House, large, sombre, redbrick Chelsea of the 1880s, belongs to Felix Hope-Nicholson, genealogist. He is a man who has a passion for Family and knows his kith and kin to the nth remove; all the ghosts have names, dates and faces. The house was designed and built in 1882 for the Victorian academician, the Hon. John Collier, who had the temerity to marry not one but two Miss Huxleys – sisters. After the first went mad and died here he went to America to marry the second (because of the illegality) and on return they were so severely snubbed by his sister-in-law, Lady Monkswell, who lived at Monkswell House on the Embankment, they felt forced to retreat to St John's Wood 'where', says Mr Hope-Nicholson, 'it didn't matter what you did. And some say it still doesn't.' Mr Hope-Nicholson's grandmother, Mrs Adrian Hope, bought the house in 1892. She believed the land originally formed part of Sir Thomas More's garden, and when disillusioned by the Vicar of Chelsea renamed it No More House. Halfway to the top of the house is Jacqueline Hope's bedroom. 'My mother married in 1916 and did up her room inspired by

Above: Felix Hope-Nicholson at a staircase window surrounded by prints and paintings of the Fitzwilliam side of the family; other walls are devoted to other parts of the family. The house remains largely unchanged since the time of his grandparents and still retains most of the original features including speaking tubes, one of which can be seen in the bottom right of this picture.

Right: The studio, with trap-door large enough to let through Academy-sized canvases. Above the fireplace a portrait of Sir Thomas Hope, to the right a family group of Mr Hope-Nicholson as a child with his mother and sisters. Beyond the fireplace an undressing-room for models and to the left of it a bunk bed so that an Admiral relation might feel at sea.

Morris Leloir's book on Cardinal Richelieu – lapis lazuli blue with gilt decorations and a four-poster bed.' There are cupboards containing twenty-one dolls and a theological library. 'Charles I and the Stuarts, children's books and dolls, the saints and theology, these were her great interests.' Objects and architecture are inseparable from people. 'My grandfather found all sorts of different bits of carving in a builder's yard at Oxford and made the fireplace in the dining-room with them. His mother turned the conservatory into a chapel. On the altar are statues of my cousin, John Ogilvy – I went to Rome for the canonisation – my cousin Philip Howard, one of the four English martyrs, and my cousin, Saint Carlo Borromeo, who is buried under the high altar in Milan Cathedral, a small bit of the hair of Bonnie Prince Charlie aged sixteen and a half, a piece of Charles I's coffin and a small bit of James II's heart.' Flanking this a bookcase bought in Oscar Wilde's bankruptcy sale, now packed with 'Britain in postcards', and, opposite, 'my mother's doll's house where a great Christmas house party is going on. All the people have names and relationships.' No doubt they are Hopes.

Left: Mr Hope-Nicholson's mother's bedroom done up in 1916 and inspired by Morris Leloir's book on Cardinal Richelieu – all lapis lazuli and gilt, the plastic floor tiles are the only new addition and look as though they have been made for the room. In the cupboards a collection of Victorian dolls such as the one at the dressing-table.

TEDDY MILLINGTON-DRAKE
A Converted Tuscan Farmhouse

Teddy Millington-Drake, painter and born traveller, drawn each year to India and Patmos to work, returns to Poggio al Pozzo, a Tuscan farmhouse circled by oak and arbutus from which you can see the towers of Siena. It is a so-called Casa Colonica, a sharecropper's house, attached to the lords of these Marches whose frontier lay along the river Arbia. Described by Dante as flowing with blood, now it flows through poplars in the valley below. Flowing over the walls of the house are motifs from his life and painting. Green and white saris hanging on a bed are a day in Kanchipuram; a bedspread means Kashmir; an ivory, Goa, whilst a brass-bound chest signals Mukalla in the Hadramawt, a city of mud palaces no longer on the

traveller's route. 'When I moved into Poggio I was still painting in an abstract way. I was writing poetry, and some of the paintings and many sets of drawings were in fact poems or phrases written across the paper or canvas. The room below was a response to a line in Baudelaire about travelling. The walls are not prepared in any way and the painting is done directly onto the whitewash with acrylic paint and pastel chalks and then fixed. The room needed something on the wall of general interest to stop it becoming just a passage. I often put a table here for dinner.' In a country of fresco, with the masterpieces of Veronese and Florence at hand, Teddy Millington-Drake's painting on the wall is particularly happy, a tradition continuing.

Above: The ante-room to the indoor dining-room or, in practical terms, a pantry where pots and dishes are housed. Here the pottery is the local splatterware seen on the top shelf, and below it a range of porcelain pots. The walls are a complete Millington-Drake painting, a contemporary version of the frescos in Palladian villas.

Right: Teddy Millington-Drake in his studio. Glass doors frame a view ready to be painted; throughout the house the windows frame extraordinary views.

Above: The kitchen. Although this is the only new building it is difficult to detect as local stone has been used, beams were exposed and the lines of the original architecture followed. The room is completely white, with white tiled floors and a central island which houses and services the electrical equipment and sink as well as being a preparation area.

Right: The huge drawing-room on the first floor stretches the length of the house in the manner of a rustic Palladian villa, with the bedrooms opening off it. At the far end, the staircase leads to a small library, once the pigeon loft. Furniture, rugs and textiles from many parts of the world glowing in many colours surround the nucleus of the room, the quiet, off-white upholstered area by the fireplace.

Left and above: The bedrooms have beds hung with cotton saris bordered in soft blues or pinks depending on the colour of the bedposts. Very simple, the saris catch the breeze, the windows frame the view and shutters alone close out the light.

MICHAEL CARDEW
Wenford Bridge Pottery in Cornwall

Michael Cardew, who died in 1983, was for his lifetime the vital force in pottery. The great potters are looking for a language of clay, for them more eloquent than words; and their pots are a philosophy in practice. Just so Wenford Bridge, the house to which Michael and his wife Mariel came after the war. It had been, by its stream and the pleasant grey bridge from which it takes its name, a source of much solace for hundreds of years, and to as many travellers, during a long life as an inn, tucked below Bodmin Moor's bald pate. A broad worn board of a bench rubbed shining black by moleskin breeches remains around what was the tap-room. The great fireplace and slate floors, the many ledges and shelves in the thickness of the wall with indispensable forgotten purposes, remain. The walls, white-washed once with initial enthusiasm are now given over to the soft fingers of smoke, age and air. In some places the plaster has settled to a mouse-brown, in others to a fresh cream glow. The patina, under watchful eyes, has been allowed to gather, and the old house has grown into the lives of the people who live there. It is impossible to detach the rooms at Wenford from Michael Cardew's ideas and life. They are as telling as a leather book of confidences. Fabrics, dyed with indigo and berries in Africa hang at the windows and are made into bedspreads and Mariel's skirt, brought back from Vume after Michael Cardew's pioneer work with African potters in the war years, all the pots and chapters in the Cardews' life, some because they celebrate the birth of a child, or because their shape celebrates a particularly successful period of potting. There is work here, also, for the detective. At tea-time Mariel alone drinks from a white china cup, a mark of her separate ideas and life. The house is none of the things that are associated with a beautiful interior, it is not full of rich objects, there are few pictures, no carpets, nor is it ascetically spartan, a nut-brown profusion of papers, books, plates, bowls and crocks of every kind makes sure of that. Yet it is one of the most satisfying places to be, the rooms fragrant with fruitwood burnt in the fire, a great tea-pot steaming, or at breakfast the covered vessels which slowly cook eggs in boiling water. The floors upstairs creak like the timbers of a ship, whilst out through the windows, when there is a firing, the open door of the kiln-shed glows red.

Michael Cardew at Wenford. Right: His writing chair on the upper floor of one of the barns; fragments of pots and of a life line the shelves. Overleaf: A corner of the kitchen, looking into the eating-room.

The industrial revolution threatened to extinguish the natural context of things made by hand, and the indigenous makers of everyday vessels, the cream pans, jugs, pitchers, plates, ovens and all that were a real part of our national identity along with it. Many people have been left out of touch with the element in an object which makes it spiritually valuable. The work of re-establishing it was pioneered by Bernard Leach at St Ives in the first decades of the century. Through the great potter Hamada, he brought Japanese influence and its unbroken tradition to mend our broken one. Michael Cardew went to St Ives one day in 1923, by all accounts a striking, tall and leonine figure, and decided to focus all the emotions that had been gathering momentum within him whilst at Oxford reading Classics and to put them, if he could, into pots.

After St Ives, he set up in an old abandoned pottery with a huge traditional bottle kiln at Winchcombe in Gloucestershire. Bearing in his mind's eye the forms and happy simplicity of pots seen and brought home from childhood visits to the pottery of Edwin Beer Fishley, whom Leach called, 'the last peasant potter', he started to develop his ideas. The process reached maturity during twenty legendary years in Africa setting up potteries in Ghana and Nigeria. There they apparently say, 'Knowledge is a baobab tree, a man cannot get his arms around it.' But Cardew embraced the country, drew strength from its beauty and found the core of unself-consciousness that a man of his intellect and education must discover if his work is not to be pastiche. The white Vume lily, with what he calls 'a kind of tropical exuberance, a sort of generosity which I learnt there', flowered in the swamps, where also lived the tall, curious, elegant birds like something from Cardew's much-loved and quoted Edward Lear that, strictly yet freely stylised, appear on plates, bowls and jars. They are the incarnations of the vital element that marks his best work, a generosity of spirit which all artists must discover in their own ways.

Left: The table laid for tea, Mariel's cup is blue and white, the egg-cookers and covered jars for sugar are at this end.

CRAIGIE AITCHISON

A Victorian Terraced House in Kennington

'Some people only like these things when they see them in here, they wouldn't want them for themselves, but they can see why I like them after a bit.' Craigie Aitchison, a Scotsman, lives and paints in a terraced house in Lambeth. His house is as peculiar to him as his vision as an artist. There is a profusion of objects, china ornaments, paper decorations, dangerous-looking electric fires in the cosy shape of scotty dogs, plaster figures bright and deliciously gaudy. He chooses everything for a sort of liveliness, a kind of poignancy, that has led him to keep a particularly merry-looking iced cake with a cherry on the top on a cake-stand in the kitchen for years without eating it.

Many of the things that surround him appear in the still-life paintings that intersperse his work on portraits and pictures using religious subjects; each kind of picture is born out of the others, in reaction and in progress, but they all share a tremendous tenderness of colour with a hard-won subtlety of form. 'I find that I start out meaning to paint the whole thing, say a flower, and then that with maybe two strokes of the same or different colours the whole thing seems to be there. I hate it when a flower turns into just a shape, but if the shape is right, the whole painting will take on a life of its own and then the shape will be completely forgotten, but it will still be there for anyone who wants to look at it for itself alone. I find in painting that it becomes a flower first very quickly, then into a shape, then back into a flower. If it does not go back then the picture is terrible.'

The house is often changed but not for the usual reasons. A bright yellow carpet will be in favour for the bathroom, later rejected for a mat with Mickey Mouse on a laughing train rushing across it, but the faded and peeling yellow

Left: Craigie Aitchison with Wainy, the Bedlington terrier, by a dark green painted door, in front of a canvas in which he features.

Above: Paint table with cheering plastic flowers.

paper with sprigs of flowers is too familiar and right to replace. It is a matter of getting things exact, a rather less exalted version of what happens on his canvases, where the canaries that live free in the house, his Bedlington terriers, friends, models, trees, flowers, Christ and landscape are worked and worked onto blazing fields of colour until they reach a still point, poised between all his feelings equally, reconciled to their place on the canvas, and by implication of that balance, to their place in the world.

Above: Fireplace with pink paint and objects – a green glass pike, small painting of a canary, curly bright gold candlestick, the Virgin with red lights.

Right: In the kitchen a black china cow tureen holds dog biscuits, things remain unmoved for years, like the paper Christmas decorations hanging from the ceiling.

ANGUS McBEAN
An Elizabethan Hall in Suffolk

Angus McBean, born in 1904, is a man of memorable beard (long and white) who lives in a Tudor manor house (long and rambling) in Suffolk. It is a house that he has largely put together with his own hands, a considerable imaginative work of restoration. His skill as artist and craftsman has been far less heralded than his skill as a photographer but it is evident that he can make, remake, create or repair anything.

Like the photographers of his ilk, Cecil Beaton and Snowdon, who acknowledge a deep debt to him, his work is in the best sense theatrical, even when it is not connected directly with the theatre. His experimental flirtation with Surrealism in photography in the thirties and forties grew from his sense of the way that our eyes understand the relationships between masses, which he loved to turn on its head. The games with appearance and reality, reference and clashes, were not sold to Harvard with the four and a half tons of glass negatives of his work; they go on, in the biggest fruit-cake known to domestic science upon his tea-table, the games of multi-coloured glass that he plays on his dressing-table, where bottles and unreasonably coloured objects are crammed together in a challenge to the established sense of good taste. He would never describe his work as accurate; it is Tudor England seen through the eyes of someone soaked in theatre of a certain date. Whatever liberties Angus McBean may have taken with Flemings Hall, the charm lies in its originality.

Built in 1380 by the Bedingfields, it was altered in 1580, when brick ends were added, and again in 1630 when gables and chimneys were added to these. Later it gained a Georgian plaster façade and portico. By the 1930s, it was falling apart, the owners were anxious to sell, could not, and so panelling,

Left: Angus McBean wears a suit that plays games with stripes and a mad hat in the hall at Flemings.

Above: Flemings Hall restored.

chimney pieces, staircases were stripped and shipped to the American market.

When in the early 1960s Angus McBean was forced into retirement by a hip operation, he could, in his own way, realise the successful man's country house dream. With friends, he found Flemings – 'more like an empty barn than a house'. Its restoration has been Angus' unstinting work. It is now listed Grade 1. 'I have given a covenant on it to the National Trust which they've accepted because of two unique features – there are three scratched sun-dials on the door, no, they don't know of another example, and the oval horse collar windows in the brick ends. We've done practically no structural alterations because we wouldn't be allowed to except pulling a Victorian chimney out of the middle. We had to do the work on the kitchen last because we couldn't have the great chimney-breast removed until we had the new roof and we couldn't afford to have the new roof because we'd spent the money we'd saved up for the new roof on the iron gates for the outside – magnificent art nouveau, made for the Duke of Westminster in Italy in 1900. We knew nothing about Tudor materials. We were high Empire and Regency when we came here.' Twenty years ago, suitably ancient materials were still available to the imaginative scavenger. No fourteenth-century wood, perhaps, but they learnt to buy from gipsy carts and, ever more picturesque, to ferret in field and hedgerow and bombed-out houses for anything Elizabethan. Things often came from more secret and official sources, a notable canopy from a bed, the sawn balusters from the bridge of an Elizabethan warship. The result is a curiously free place where the imagination can live well, where Angus McBean has re-made the past according to his image of how it should have been, yesterday all mixed up with today. Before we know it we are opening a door into Surrealism again, at the end of one of these corridors with painted gothic *trompe l'oeil* and ancient timbers and a photograph of Vivien Leigh. The effect is conscious. 'No Old Master paintings, no really grand

Above: View from the landing at Flemings Hall, lath and plaster restored. The staircase balusters were formerly at sea doing service in an Elizabethan warship.

Right: The Owl bedroom goes overboard for carving, owls stuffed, and Minton jugs.

furniture, plate not silver – just a good effect. And pottery looks better with oak than the grandest porcelain.' The pottery is in decorative collections from nineteenth-century English factories – Minton corn jugs in the Owl bedroom, Spode Etruscan-ware massed along one wall in the kitchen. Pictures are motley, powerful photographs of once and famous stars, glass, tinsel, owls, cats, fibreglass, a portrait of Angus in brocade dressing-gown and nightcap by the Russian painter Marevna. In the great hall the screen beam is revealed, the ceiling roughly plastered, the fire-place a marquetry of linenfold and pilasters, the floor traditional Suffolk stone flags. One bookcase wall has recessed jib doors. There are very theatrical crimson painted leather curtains. All woodwork is a miracle of extended, shortened, mixed, matched and dovetailed panelling. On showing one guest to his room Angus remarked, 'I made that bed this morning.' 'Oh, we all have to do that sort of thing nowadays,' said the guest, quite unaware that McBean meant made, as in built. His skills were nurtured in the atmosphere of the theatre and he has given that atmosphere back through those same skills, in the restoration of Elizabethan tombs (eighteen in the Tollemache church), masks and puppets, pictures of unlikely fibreglass, the props for his photography, silk-screened wallpapers for Flemings, Beatles record sleeves (the first and the last) and major projects of decoration such as the Academy cinema in 1954, more wallpapers, ironwork, carpets, china. He is a photographer who has always known his craft, his pictures were riddles, 'How did he do that?' people asked. 'Although I had this extraordinary chance, that I was number one theatre photographer for thirty years during one of the four great periods of English theatre, I would say that my best piece of work, my most important work, is this house.'

Left: Set piece of McBean colour sense, against a startling paisley wallpaper. All the colours belong to the same acid register of raspberry, lemon, turquoise, appropriate to the hardness of glass.

Above: A cast of Stafford pot figures, Architecture, Medicine and one pair of Lady Hamiltons by Ralph Wood the Elder, circa 1800, perform on a table in the Great Hall, their colours echoed in those of an orchid.

GRACE CODDINGTON
Two White Rooms in Fulham

Needing space, Grace, Senior Fashion Editor of *Vogue*, has let the walls of her small flat dissolve in cream and white paint. Over the years she has taken away not added, and the rooms are not so much decorated as stripped bare, then dressed according to her mood. When time and fortune allow, a wall goes or a floor gets renewed with pale, bleached boards. Travels bring objects that find favour for a season and bring their inspiration too: a sofa got up in laundered Chinese manner, a romantic and temporary mosquito net to drape the bed like a Raj house in Ceylon with its slow, white propeller fan blowing curtains, and a red-stitched New England quilt like something from a picture by Andrew Wyeth.

An untidy childhood and a life of using her eyes to judge the cut and hang of fabric has softened the edges of a strictly disciplined arrangement. Tidiness is at the heart of this pleasure, in the reassuring smell of washed and ironed cotton, the casual neatness of pleats on the sofa and bed, as at home as on a skirt. But the past has not been banished. Elsewhere in the house are photographs from past magazines, memories of New Mexico in a print by Georgia O'Keefe, colours and shapes that found particular favour for some fashionable spell: Calvin Klein lacquer red, the stylish shapes of Art Deco. All is the result of definite choices like the bookcase with its glass-doored shelves, made to fit their place, purpose and owner.

Above: The small sitting-room, pale and simple. The sofa is loosely dressed in white cotton, with deep-pleated frill, and lace armrests. The cabinet along the back wall was specially commissioned and made by Andrew Mortada, reminiscent of display cases in old-fashioned drapers.

Right: The tiny bedroom, 10' by 8'. Neat use of attic space with the double bed fitted beneath the slope of the roof. A quilt stands in as headboard. The mosquito net is more decorative than practical.

THE CARRINGTONS
A Cottage on the Berkshire Downs

The taste of Bloomsbury was always bound up with books and ideas. Its houses favoured a particular mix of personal stamp and Englishness, like the visual wit of Hogarth, the gaunt with the lively, the dignified with the odd. Noel and Catherine Carrington's house, tucked in the Vale of the White Horse, built in local sarsen stone with brick coigns, has windows and a spirit very much to that taste; eighteenth-century Gothick with a hint of beehive in shape, punning with a Holm Oak clipped for the purpose. Dora Carrington, Noel's sister, was responsible for making two houses liveable for Lytton Strachey, whom she loved. Her taste was a natural expression of herself, like her handwriting (Virginia Woolf called it 'my idea of the perfect hand'). The first house was the mill at Tidmarsh, with dressers crowded with pottery, some brought laboriously back from Spain by Gerald Brenan, a writer living in Andalucia out of a rucksack, but the mill proved too damp for Lytton. The second was Ham Spray where she made a library for him with a door covered in *trompe l'oeil* books and little pleated lampshades of marbled paper, like endpapers.

Noel Carrington has lived a life of distinguished publishing in England and India – thereby treading in the heat and dust of his father's footsteps who built a railway with the East India Company, before settling in the same landscapes that his sister loved and painted: long downs with stands of beeches like a picture by Paul Nash, her contemporary. Catherine, too, painted. They knew Lytton as juniors, as visitors to Olympus. 'When Noel was in London I was alone with him. I remember him once telling me all about the life of bees, it was fascinating, he knew such a lot about them.' Later Stanley Spencer would show the Carringtons' own children bees from the hive in the garden, picking them up in his hands. It is a spontaneous affection for particular colours and things that marks the Carringtons' house as it marked Dora Carrington's pictures. The fairground zest of pink lustre pottery, plates painted with cockerels, unmatched saucers, of unrigid rules, a freedom of thought. Like the drawings that speckle Carrington's letters which have a facility of line the counterpart of her self, their house is full of chance and choice always judged by a painter's eye.

Above: The Carringtons' eighteenth-century Gothick house in Berkshire, built of local stone and distinguished by its curious beehive-shaped windows.

Right: Bedroom, a lesson in simplicity, the painted door leading on to another, the choice of colour harmonious to both rooms. Just the right amount of furniture and each piece simple, the chair came from Strachey's house 'Ham Spray'. The curtains unlined and sashed back.

Below: Detail from the sitting-room; reflected in the mirror over the fireplace, a painting by Dora Carrington, 'Farm at Watendlath'. She wrote in 1921, 'I sat and drew a white cottage and a barn, sitting on a little hill until it grew cold.' A painting of a cottage for a small house.

Right: The kitchen. Dresser painted by Catherine Carrington and filled with plates, all for use, the middle row French, the rest English. A kitchen where everything is shown and all is used; well designed objects need never be hidden away.

DAVID HOCKNEY
A London Studio

Artists are not in business to collect their own paintings, and David Hockney's studio is full of his pictures because it is in his place of work. 'I don't want to sit back and look at the finished ones, I'm only interested in what I'm working on.' To this end the furniture in the studio is concentrated around the easel, and apart from a leather sofa, the furniture has an air of being temporarily placed, light garden chairs that remind him of summer and the sun on deck, since Hockney is famous for disliking the English climate and retreats to California's better weather. This studio has travelled with him, the style has not changed even though he has moved several times, since what he needs for painting, light, space and organisation, have remained constant.

'I have no possessions really, I could live in a hotel, I don't paint London. I paint in the studio, but the outside I ignore. Yet when I'm in California I paint the outside as well; I paint everything. I love looking at it; I find Los Angeles a very beautiful city, it's one of the few places where the architecture was designed to be looked at, at fifteen miles an hour. In Europe, buildings are made to be looked at when you walk past them or up to them, or when you are standing still.' Hockney has always had an eye for the witty and a tremendous personal chic. He is always the first with new gadgets, the tiny camera, the disposable watch, the toy of the moment, and this is part of the talent for enjoyment which is the principal feature of his work. Perhaps that is why Hockney has always looked a little out-

Above: The pinboard in the studio, 'a big, visual diary', an aide-memoire and a place where paintings sometimes begin. Most of the photographs are by Hockney.

Right: Hockney in his bathroom, reflected in the shower screen which is made from mirrored plastic sheeting and never seems to steam up.

rageous, literally looking on the bright side, in yellow and blue stripes, with unmatched socks, even unmatched shoes, to jog perceptions, to draw attention, not specifically to himself, but to the fact that there are more ways than convention suggests to look at things.

But Hockney is no revolutionary, he works at the speed of our culture, surfing and focusing on the ideas thrown up by current events, ideas and people, and our response to the art of the past. In some ways Hockney's paintings and drawings are a critique of the revolutions of others, explaining Picasso, Stravinsky, Mozart, by putting them on the stage, both literally, in his designs for opera, and on the stage of public acceptance.

In the studio, mirrors reflect many views of the artist and his world simultaneously. 'My image is quite separate from me,' he says, but the tulips in vases in a million houses would not look as they do if Hockney had not showed them to us in that way. If a measure of an artist is that he changes the way we see the world, then perhaps Hockney is sure of a place in the history of how we see our surroundings, his studio the blue-print for a style.

Above: The deep blue screen, a backdrop for portraits and Hockney at tea; the wicker furniture, painted green, has the atmosphere of a transatlantic liner.

Right: The large top floor studio, drenched with light from the wall-length windows and skylight. Even the leather sofa faces the easel and the work in hand, paints are neatly shelved. The paintings on the walls from left to right 'Café in Luxor' (1978), two untitled still lives (1977 and 1970), and an unfinished profile of Peter Schlesinger seated on the same chair as that in the foreground.

FARINGDON

An Eccentric Country House in Oxfordshire

The lawn sweeps across to the town church. At the striking of a clock a clattering cloud of once-white doves, now pale-blue, yellow and lavender, go down to Buscot Woods below Robert Heber-Percy's house.

Faringdon House, one of the most elegant of late-Georgian manors, was built for Henry James Pye, a laureate of minor powers whose first birthday Ode, 1790, alluded all too often to 'feathered vocal groves and feathered choirs'. But there is nothing bird-brained or slight about Faringdon. The architecture sits with total assurance upon its site, the structure sits within, particularly the marvellous staircase hall, a masterpiece of unswerving geometry. The robust proportions of the rooms allow a freedom of fancy in the decorations. The imagination that Robert Heber-Percy inherited with the house was that of Lord Berners, the delight of the muses and his friends; composer, man of ludicrous letters, incapable of total seriousness, but blessed with talents that everybody enjoyed, and free with them.

Faringdon has been the scene of high-brows and high-jinks, the Marchesa Casati arrived with a snake or two ('Yes, but what does it have for breakfast, My Lord?'). Stravinsky came, Gertrude Stein, Rex Whistler, Frederick Ashton . . . so many of the people who were leading twentieth-century preconceptions a merry dance. And the house fitted them all. The games still go on, the chandelier hanging *outside* the front door, the clockwork watchdog, the spoof pictures of false moustaches facing masterpieces, the air of tongue-in-cheek and flight of fancy, a four-poster with crystal posts, like ice, or the swimming-pool with rearing Elizabethan wyverns, designed by Robert Heber-Percy to sit like something from Loch Ness on the surface of the water.

Faringdon is a delicious balance, the architecture is debunked by the frivolity of its owners, the owners are tempered by the classicism of the house; they are a perfect background for one another.

Above: Robert Heber-Percy with a flight of his coloured pigeons, in front of Faringdon House, an elegant late-Georgian manor.

Right: The hall seen from the front door. The double staircase, much admired by Pevsner, has its back to the entrance. The symmetry of the architecture dictates a similar symmetry in the arrangement of furniture and paintings.

Top: The orangery with fish pool in front of which the centrepiece is the bust of an Indian Army General.

Above: The swimming-pool designed by Robert Heber-Percy, the waterline marked by a pair of rare Elizabethan Wyverns.

Right: Inside the orangery plants vie for space with family portraits, bentwood furniture and a Georgian looking glass, painted white.

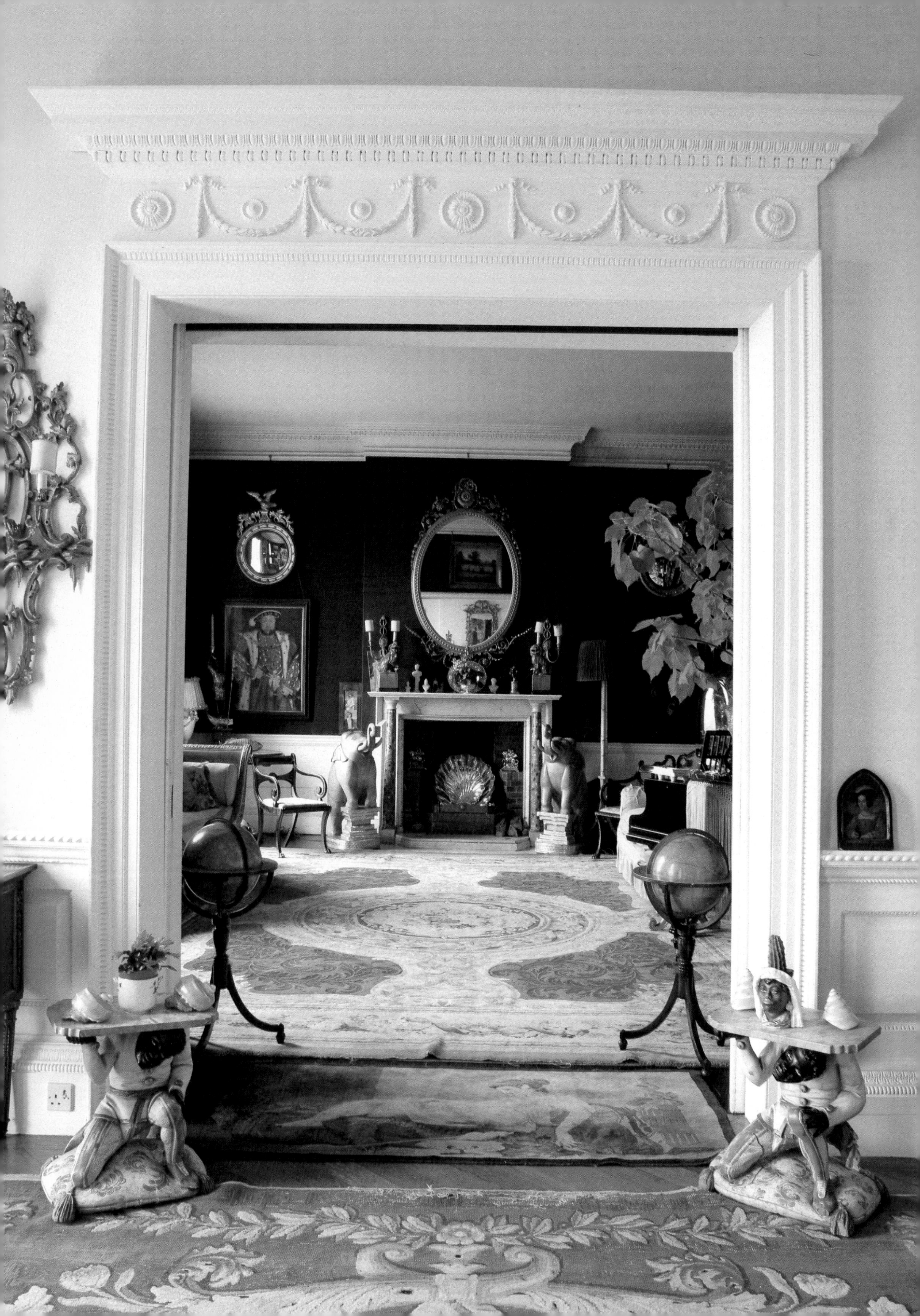

Left: The double drawing-room, one half dark and the other pale. In the distance some recently acquired elephants, a portrait of Henry VIII and piles of embroidered Victorian cushions. At either side of the door blackamoors stand in as tables.

Above: A detail from the pale end of the drawing-room with Chippendale furniture and a moustache collage done by a grandchild. The wicker fish bag was left on the chair by that grandchild's grandmother some twenty years ago. It has not been moved since.

ERTÉ
A Château Outside Paris

Through the stuffy, crowded and unromantic suburbs of Paris, not far beyond, stands a château behind forbidding gates. It is no masterpiece, a Victorian merchant's delusion of grandeur with too much of the ugly villa about it that he should have left behind. But through the front door lies a kingdom unlike any other, a fantasy world of glass and pearls and furs and skins, of horn and hide and shiny, dreadful turquoise fur.

It is the work of Erté, he of the dazzling ideas for the stage, of the uniquely theatrical image, the perfectly finished illustrations, magazine covers, costumes, the idealised, decorative female form. Women have been an accessory to his fertile imagination since the twenties when, as Roland Barthes put it, 'Erté shaped the implicit form of the woman today, born from the battles for emancipation,

feminine, not in her consciousness, but only in her dress, her hairstyle, her jewels: a woman disguised as a woman...' In the designs for the château, Erté shows his colours in typically untypical fashion. Born in pre-revolutionary Russia, all troikas and frozen rivers, he broke from the rigid notions that his naval family had for his future, headed for Paris, the glass of fashion, and work for the great couturier Poiret. His vision proved too personal, and he entered his own world in which he has lived successfully ever since. 'I never start anything until I have planned it in my head. Inspiration only comes when you have really worked and thought about what you are doing.' Behind his precise, studied appearance, his faultless *politesse* ('The only hypocrisy I believe in is politeness'), lurk enormously extravagant plumed ideas, like the interior of the château,

Above: Erté, the theatrical designer. He was born in pre-revolution Russia, his real name is Romain de Tirtoff, he made up the name Erté from his initials.

Right: Reflections multiply in the fantasy world of Erté's dining-room where the domed ceiling is mirrored and hung with a chandelier and cobwebs of crystals. It is difficult to tell where image begins and reality ends. The room is shown upside down to show Erté the right way up, seated with friends at a marble dining table.

behind its conventional front. Inside, neither he nor the château are remotely restrained by taste. He has mastered the selfish art of extravagance by a generosity of wit and because he likes things overdone. The result is overpowering and has total authority.

In a mixture of Scottish baronial nightmare and whimsy, of black lacquer furniture and grotto shell chairs, of bone and horn thrones, fur ceilings and Wedgwood tea pots, musical chairs that sing when you sit on them and feathered birds chirping in a sedan chair, the château gazes at itself in mirrors. The entrance hall is a pale brown marble cave where looking glasses have barnacled surrounds of Babylonian whelks and tiger cowries, scallops and queen conches. The grandfather clocks, too, look as though they have been hauled up from the deep with heavy debts to Neptune. They were made, along with much of the furniture, by J. Antony Redmile in London, and Erté has lent more Rococo liberties to them. In the drawing-room the seats are hung with the artefacts of seals, reindeer, yak and moose, the elephant tusk and the fluted horn of the gazelle, at once horrific, splendid, sad and pagan. The fireplace is cavernous, the windows are stained goatskin so that, once closed, you are sealed in a fur and bone world, tended by suits of armour, visors down, who bear tea-trays on their clenched fists. It looks uninhabitable, and uninhabited, a furry tomb. The dining-room could scarcely be more different. A cool kaleidoscope, a maze of mirrors that reflects crystal and gold to infinity, looping pearls until the whole room wears a necklace, there is no way of seeing where reality ends and fantasy begins. But with Erté you are never sure.

Right: The drawing-room, a conservationist's nightmare, a world of fur and horn, where shutters are covered and lined with goatskin. Baronial Gothic furniture of horn and leather made by J. Anthony Redmile with further fantasy by Erté, a room where suits of armour, complete with ostrich plumes, act as footmen and hold absurd trays for tea. The twentieth-century technology of stereo cases which revolve at a touch. A place where Beauty meets Beast.

Acknowledgements

We are indebted to the writers upon and from whose accounts in *Vogue* many of the texts in this book were written:

Joan Juliet Buck, Roderick Cameron, the late David Carritt, Bruce Chatwin, Polly Devlin, James Fox, Christopher Gibbs, William Green, Nicholas Haslam, Selina Hastings, Elizabeth Lambert, Gavin Stamp and Antonia Williams.

We would like to thank the Duchess of Devonshire for the use of remarks from her book *The House, A Portrait of Chatsworth*, Macmillan, 1982 and Lesley Blanch for passages from her book *Pierre Loti*, Collins, 1983 on which the account of Pierre Loti, A Writer's House in Rochefort is based.

Photographic Credits

Page 2 Tessa Traeger; *8, 11* Derry Moore; *12, 14* David Montgomery; *15–23* James Mortimer; *24–31* Christopher Simon Sykes; *32–35* Derry Moore; *36–39* Snowdon; *40–43* Lucinda Lambton; *44–47* David Montgomery; *48–51* Snowdon; *52–55* David Montgomery; *56–59* James Mortimer; *60* Joe Gaffney (portrait); *60–65* Snowdon; *66–67* Derry Moore; *68–71* Christopher Drake; *72* David Montgomery; *74–79* Christopher Simon Sykes; *80–85* Snowdon; *86–93* Steve Lovi; *94–97* Derry Moore; *98–101* Snowdon; *102–107* David Montgomery; *108–113* Eric Boman; *114–117* Derry Moore; *118–123* Christopher Simon Sykes; *124–129* Steve Lovi; *130–145* Derry Moore; *146–149* Snowdon; *150–155* Christopher Simon Sykes; *156–159* Kenneth Griffiths